Markets, Fair Trade
and the Kingdom of God

Markets, Fair Trade and the Kingdom of God

Essays to Celebrate
Traidcraft's 21st Birthday

EDITED BY

Peter Johnson and Chris Sugden

Traidcraft
Fighting poverty through trade

regnum

First published 2001 by Regnum Books International
in association with
Paternoster Publishing, PO Box 300, Carlisle, CA3 0QS, UK
and
PO Box 1047, Waynesboro, GA 30830-2047, USA

Regnum Books International
PO Box 70, Oxford, OX2 6HB, UK

17951 Cowan, Irvine, California, 92714 USA

José Marmol 1734, 1602 Florida, Buenos Aires, Argentina

PO Box 76, Akropong-Akuapem, Ghana

Post Bag number 21, Vasant Kunj, New Delhi 110057, India

c/o Dr Hwa Yung, Seminaria Theologi Malaysia,
PO Box 175, 70720 Seremban, Malaysia

04 03 02 01 00   7 6 5 4 3 2 1

British Library Cataloguing in Publication Data
A catalogue record for this book is available from the British Library.

ISBN 1-870345-19-3

Typeset by Reesprint,
Radley, Oxfordshire, OX14 3AJ, UK

Printed and bound by Cox and Wyman,
Reading, Berkshire, RG1 8EX, UK

TO TRAIDCRAFT'S FAIR TRADERS,

PARTNERS AND PRODUCERS

Contents

Introduction   ix
Peter Johnson and Chris Sugden

List of Contributors   xii

Part I: Some Bigger Issues

1   Fair Trade as Christian Mission   3
Chris Sugden

2   Renewing the Market Place   25
Peter Johnson

3   Poverty-Reducing Development Strategies: 39
Accepted and Neglected Challenges
Deryke Belshaw

Part II: Traidcraft's Experience and Future

4   Beginnings and Intentions   69
Richard Adams

5   Traidcraft's Christian Basis and its Relationship   82
with its Overseas Partners
Philip Angier

6   Traidcraft and its Staff   90
Yvonne Dare

7   Traidcraft and its Fair Traders   106
Campbell Grant

8   Traidcraft's Christian Basis and the Secular   117
        Market Place
        Stuart Raistrick

9   Traidcraft and the Churches   130
        Margaret Masson

10   Resurrection and Hope: Traidcraft's Future   141
        David Nussbaum

Appendix One

What is Traidcraft?   150

Appendix Two

Traidcraft's Foundation Principles   152

Traidcraft's Contact Addresses   156

Introduction

Peter Johnson and Chris Sugden

Traidcraft is twenty-one years old. It grew out of a passionate desire to give some practical expression to principles of justice and love in international trade, and thereby to provide an opportunity to poor people in various parts of the world to compete on fair terms with dignity, and to value themselves and their products.

Over the past two decades much has been achieved. Traidcraft has given leadership to many in this country who shared the same passion as its founders, and who welcomed the opportunity to do something that rewarded the work and initiative of poor people. It has tried hard to apply Christian principles in its own activities and management. Traidcraft's name is now well known among consumers; new product lines and advisory services have been successfully introduced; cafédirect has been launched and fair trade products are on sale in supermarkets; the organisation has grown significantly in size; governments have turned to Traidcraft for advice; lobbying for company law reform has been robust; Shared Interest has been launched and developed; and social accounting has been introduced and promoted.

The environment within which Traidcraft has developed has been in a constant state of change since 1979. While its founders had been nurtured by the idealism of Martin Luther King, the Civil Rights Struggle in the USA of the sixties, and anti-war protests, 1979, the year Traidcraft was established, saw the introduction of Thatcherism, a radically different way of approaching economic and social life. On the business front, globalisation and computerisation have proceeded rapidly; some countries have seen enormous economic progress, while others have experienced stagnation or decline; and consumer tastes and available technologies have undergone significant change. No let-up to these developments is in sight. This continuing process of change means that Traidcraft cannot stay still; it must adapt its operations in the light of new developments, while remaining true to its underlying vision, and maintaining that passion for justice and love that first led to its setting up.

It is against the background of thankfulness to God for what has been achieved, and of an awareness that, under God, we need to move on as the environment around us changes, that these essays have been written by members of Traidcraft's leadership, past and present, to celebrate Traidcraft's coming of age. They are offered to inform the wider Traidcraft community of Traidcraft's Christian roots and commitment; to challenge Christians to embrace a holistic understanding of Christian discipleship as necessarily including justice; and stimulate all Christians in their business and work callings to see justice as part of their witness. They all reflect the struggles that arise from seeking to express such discipleship. Most of the contributions come from the joint meeting of the Traidcraft Foundation Trustees, and the members of the joint Board of Traidcraft plc and Traidcraft Exchange in the Spring of 2000.

The essays divide conveniently into two groups. The essays in Part I provide a broader context for Traidcraft's activities, and consider three key aspects. In chapter 1, Chris Sugden examines fair trade as Christian mission. Chapter 2, by Peter Johnson, looks at the opportunities for bringing Christian values into market operations. Finally, Deryke Belshaw sets a wider framework of poverty-focused development strategy within which fair trade can be located and assessed, and discusses the increasing opportunities for church involvement in development activities.

In Part II, specific aspects of Traidcraft's past, current and future operations are considered. Chapter 4 by Richard Adams looks back at the formation of Traidcraft and reflects on its development over the last two decades. Philip Angier examines Traidcraft's Christian basis and considers its links with its overseas partners in chapter 5. In chapter 6, Yvonne Dare explores the issues which arise in the management of personnel in an organisation that seeks to be Christian based. Chapter 7, by Campbell Grant, looks at Traidcraft's relationships with its representatives and in chapter 8, Stuart Raistrick considers the ways in which Traidcraft interacts with the secular market place. Margaret Masson examines the interface between Traidcraft and the churches in chapter 9. The final chapter, by David Nussbaum, offers some reflections on the way ahead for Traidcraft. The Appendices provide an introduction to Traidcraft and reproduce the Foundation Principles (revised 1999).

The essays embody a variety of views. Inevitably there are tensions, even generation gaps, between people who have the same vision to work with the poor for a better world, and profoundly different approaches to achieving it. Some of those tensions and divisions have inevitably been reflected in Traidcraft's work, and are reflected in these pages. The views expressed in each chapter are those of the contributor who wrote it; they are not necessarily shared by the editors or the other contributors.

Traidcraft began with a radical vision and the impetuosity of those who wanted to change the world. We have had some considerable successes, but it is important that we retain that first passion, passion not for our own systems, or organisation, or methods in developing fair trade, but simply a passion, born of the Holy Spirit, to see God's will done on earth.

This volume would not have been possible without the ready co-operation and dedication of the contributors. As editors, we are very grateful for the way in which they found the time in busy schedules to meet tight deadlines and to respond to our comments and suggestions for change. We would also like to offer our heartfelt thanks to the many past and current employees, representatives and friends of Traidcraft who have not contributed directly to this volume, but who nevertheless have played an absolutely vital role in Traidcraft's work over the years. Without them, this book would not have been published.

List of Contributors

Richard Adams was founding Managing Director of Traidcraft.

Philip Angier is Chief Executive of Traidcraft.

Deryke Belshaw is Professor Emeritus of Development Studies at the University of East Anglia, Dean of Development Studies at the Oxford Centre for Mission Studies and a former Trustee of Traidcraft.

Yvonne Dare is Director of Human Resources of Traidcraft.

Campbell Grant is Director of Institutional Fundraising for Traidcraft.

Peter Johnson is a Professor in the University of Durham Business School and a Trustee of Traidcraft.

Margaret Masson teaches at the University of Durham and is a Board member of Traidcraft.

David Nussbaum is the Finance Director of Oxfam and Chair of the Board of Traidcraft.

Stuart Raistrick is Chair of Helix Arts and Company Secretary of the Shared Interest Society and of the North-East Civic Trust. He has been a Board member of Traidcraft since 1994, and was its Joint Chair from 1997 to 1999.

Chris Sugden is Director of Academic Affairs at the Oxford Centre for Mission Studies and Chair of the Foundation Trustees of Traidcraft.

Part I

Some Bigger Issues

Chapter One

Fair Trade as Christian Mission[1]

Chris Sugden

How does Traidcraft express Christian mission? This chapter will first reflect on the Bible in the light of that question, and then reflect on the activity of Traidcraft and Alternative Trade Organisations in the light of the Bible.

HOW DID JESUS ENGAGE IN MISSION?

Jesus is our pattern for mission. When he appeared to the disciples on Easter evening in the locked upper room, he said that 'As the Father sent me, so send I you' (Jn. 20:21). The pattern for Jesus' mission was to announce and demonstrate the Kingdom of God.

Mark 1:14 introduces Jesus' ministry as announcing that *the Kingdom of God has drawn near.* Matthew 10:5–8 records Jesus' commission to the disciples to 'proclaim the good news: The Kingdom of heaven has come near. Cure the sick, raise the dead, cleanse the lepers, cast out demons.' The Kingdom of God fulfils God's purposes in creation. It will come in its fulness when Jesus returns and brings history to its climax. It is where God's will is done 'on earth as it is in heaven'. Jesus announced that the reality (but not full extent) of the Kingdom had come to earth through his ministry. His mission is, therefore, about more than personal relationships. It is about enabling God's will to be done in all areas of human activity in managing the creation. Proclaiming the good news of the Kingdom involved word and deed. For example, Luke 8:1–3 records that Jesus went through cities and villages proclaiming and bringing the good news of the Kingdom of God. Luke adds that both the disciples and a number of women went around with him. This was an extraordinary demonstration of the Kingdom, for it was against Jewish tradition and custom for men and women to mix freely in public. These women included people from different social 'strata'. The men could not have done their work without these many women who provided for Jesus and the disciples out of their resources. So Jesus' Kingdom activity demonstrated God's will in the arena of male/female relationships.

Jesus' ministry, was *to bring 'good news to the poor'* (Lk. 4:18) In the Bible, the term 'poor' means what it means in common sense English – the economically and socially disadvantaged. When John the Baptist sent messengers to Jesus to find if he is the one to come or whether they should look for someone else, Jesus answered, 'Go and tell John what you have seen and heard: the blind receive their sight, the lame walk, the lepers are cleansed, the deaf hear, the dead are raised, the poor have good news brought to them' (Lk. 7:22). Jesus is referring to those whose physical conditions in life are of deprivation and suffering when he refers to the blind, the lame, the lepers, the deaf and the dead – and the poor. An international biblical study concluded, 'The poor (in scripture) refers to the manual worker who struggles to survive on a day to day basis, the destitute cowering as a beggar, the one reduced to meekness, the one brought low ... those weak and tired from carrying heavy burdens, and very often the common people.'[2] The 'poor in spirit' refers to those who because of their condition in this world are dependent on or have turned to God. The term does not refer to spiritual deadness, atheism or humility. For many poor people the good news of Jesus has been that in societies where they are marginalised and treated as outcast 'nobodies', they can have an identity as daughters and sons of God through the free grace of God in Jesus.

What then is the good news to the poor? It is that:

> ... God has established his Kingdom of righteousness and peace through the incarnation, ministry, atoning death and resurrection of his Son Jesus Christ. The Kingdom fulfils God's purpose in creation by bringing wholeness to humanity and the whole creation. In the Kingdom, people receive by grace alone a new

status before God and people, a new dignity and worth as his daughters and sons, and empowerment by his Spirit to be stewards of creation and servants of one another in a new community. The Kingdom will come in its fulness in a new heaven and earth only when Jesus returns.

Those who respond to this good news who are poor in the material sense or powerless are empowered by the Spirit and served by other members of the Kingdom community to experience full humanity as stewards of God's creation. The non-poor who become poor-in-spirit receive a true dignity replacing false pride in riches and are liberated to be truly human with a passion for justice for the poor. They are to trust in the power of God's Spirit which enables them to serve rather than to control. They enter a new family that accepts them for who they are rather than for their achievements – in material prosperity or status. The task of evangelisation among the majority of the unreached who are poor will be carried out primarily by those who are poor, with appropriate support from those economically advantaged who are poor in spirit.[3]

Jesus sought what can be called the 'frontier' of the good news of the Kingdom with the situation of different groups of people as he met them. For each group of people, the question we could imagine Jesus asking was, 'If the Kingdom of God came tomorrow morning, what would change most significantly for this group of people?' Jesus took the Pharisees to task for concentrating on the petty details of the law to the exclusion of its real concerns for justice, mercy and peace (Matt. 23:23). The law had been given to Israel to ensure that the injustice that they had experienced in Pharaoh's Egypt was not repeated in the promised land. It was given 'that there will be no one in need among you' (Dt. 15:4). But the Pharisees turned the law into a means of excluding people they described as 'sinners' from the society of Israel. For the sick, the most significant change was to their fatalism. They were led to believe that they were under God's curse and that nothing could be done for them. Jesus tells those he heals that their faith has healed them (Matt. 9:22; Mk. 5:34, 10:52).

The Kingdom of God fulfils God's purposes in creation. The New Testament looks forward to the time when the kingdoms of this world have become the Kingdom of our Lord (Rev.

11:15) and when the kings of the earth bring the glory of the nations into the city of God (Rev. 21:24). The kingdom of God when Jesus returns will mean a new heaven and a new earth where righteousness will be at home (Rev. 21:1).

One of God's purposes in creation was that *men and women together would be stewards of the creation.* The meaning of the term 'image of God' (Gen. 1:27–28) is that humanity images or represents the invisible God who owns the earth by acting as manager and tenant. God commands those who image him to be fruitful and have dominion over the earth on his behalf. This dominion is not unrestrained tyranny; it is to mirror the dominion of God, who in scripture is a caring shepherd king. All should be stewards of creation. Stewardship requires access to resources. Lack of access to useful and productive work undermines people's humanity. An increasing awareness by individuals of their responsibilities as stewards is seen in their ability to take responsibility for decisions and to use resources efficiently. All who are responsible for the stewardship of creation should also receive the fruits of creation. This stewardship in Genesis is set in the context of the family, of the command to men and women to be fruitful and multiply (Gen. 1:27–28).

The fall has impaired our ability to be stewards. The corruption of the relationships between people and between people and the environment is an expression of the corruption of their relationship with God.

God's action to bring salvation to the world began with poor Hebrew migrant slaves in Egypt. He delivered them and gave them a land and a law to live by. The law's purpose was that the oppression of Pharoah's Egypt should not obtain among them. But, recognising the reality of poverty, the law made provisions for loans for the poor. A zero-interest loan was available and if the principal was not repaid by the end of six years the balance would be forgiven (Ex. 22:25; Lev. 25:35–38; Dt. 15:1–11).

John Mason comments:

> The biblical provision of a compassionate loan provides assistance to the able-bodied without either unnecessarily stigmatising them or creating conditions ripe for excessive dependency upon assistance programmes. A loan recognises that the weaker family unit remains a productive component of the community

which can, with time and some reduced consumption, very probably take care of its economic responsibilities. Use of a loan protects against the development of excessive dependence upon assistance. A loan requires less community concern to monitor; the loan obligation serves as a pressure to work harder rather than to shirk. The compassionate aspects of the loan indicate the community's acknowledgement that the weaker family had little control over its difficulties, and that the community is willing to assist. (So) it is good for the social-psychological health of the adversely affected *beth'ab* [father's house].[4]

Implicit in this provision is the concern that people should be protected in their ability to be stewards of the creation. Part of our expression of salvation in this world should involve the demonstration of the recovery of our responsibility for creation and enable people to recover their position as managers of creation. Paul indicates that God's purpose is that Christian disciples be 'conformed to the image of his [God's] Son' (Rom. 8:29). Jesus is the second Adam, the true image of God, the true steward of the earth, the one who shows us how to manage the earth. Disciples of Jesus should know and show how to manage the earth best. When God's purpose is fulfilled, the kings of the earth will bring the glory of the nations into the city of God (Rev. 21:22). The best of humanity's stewardship will be present in the new earth – transformed but recognisable. In obeying God's will for humanity, we should also seek to enable human beings to be stewards and managers of creation. And this purpose will find fulfilment in the new heaven and new earth.

Thus Christian mission is reversing the effects of the Fall. It points out the integral effects of human sin in distorting all people's relationships, demonstrates the nature of a right relationship with God in restoring stewardship and shows the necessity of a relationship with Christ so that people be servants of one another. It demonstrates the nature of sin, the nature of God redeeming creation, and points to the need for allegiance to Christ.

In obedience to a biblical understanding of mission, Christian mission throughout the Two-Thirds World has been a response to the needs of the whole person to be treated with dignity, to exercise stewardship and to be able to support their family. The very start of the nineteenth-century mission activity of the western churches in Africa was to repay the debt to Africa incurred by the slave trade. According to the president of the World Bank, James Wolfensohn, the current standing of the Christian church is that it is *de facto* the world's largest Non-Governmental Organisation, and, according to the World Health Organisation, the church is the world's largest provider of health care. It reaches into almost every village on earth.

The gospel is shared in many ways in scripture. I want to highlight two. First, Jesus shared the gospel with those who were 'outsiders' by means of parables. Jesus says, 'To you [disciples] has been given the secret of the Kingdom of God, but for those outside everything comes in parables; in order that "they may indeed look, but not perceive, and may indeed listen, but not understand" ' (Mk 4:10–12). I suggest that *the parable is a form of communication particularly suited to those who do not want to hear.* The classic parable is that which Nathan told King David (2 Sam. 12). Imagine Nathan's problem. The King of Israel had both committed adultery with Bathsheba and murdered her husband by proxy. Anyone who openly rebuked David would have a sharply decreased life expectancy. Nathan constructed a drama in which David had to make a judgement. He flattered David by explaining a problem to him, of the man with many flocks who stole a poor man's one ewe lamb to prepare a meal for a guest. David pronounced that 'the man who has done this deserves to die.' David committed himself. He could not turn back. Nathan only had to say 'You are the man.' Jesus' parables create a drama in which the listeners are asked to make a judgement. They find that they have judged themselves and cannot turn back. They will never be the same again. They do not come to faith at once – but they have gone one step along the road.

The gospel is also shared in scripture through *event and explanation*. An event takes place which someone gets up to explain. When the Spirit comes on the Day of Pentecost, the disciples appear on the streets of Jerusalem speaking all the languages of the Mediterranean. How can this be explained? Some suggest that they are drunk. Peter explains that Jesus has been raised by God and sent his Spirit in fulfilment of the prophecy of Joel. In Acts 3 the same process happens. Peter and John heal a lame man at the Beautiful Gate of the Temple. He runs into the Temple praising God. Peter explains that this marvel was through Jesus whom they crucified and God raised from the dead. Peter and John get arrested, but only to get the chance for giving a further explanation, this time to the very Jewish rulers who had had Jesus put to death a few weeks earlier.

HOW TRAIDCRAFT EXPRESSES CHRISTIAN MISSION

The activities of Traidcraft faithfully express some of these biblical patterns today.

Judith Sugden writes: 'Fair trade is not a general theory of trade.... Fair trade is ... a pragmatic response to unsatisfactory outcomes of the market by changing the nature of trading relationships.... The fact there is no theory (of fair trade) indicates the essential pragmatism of fair trade.'[5]

Fair trade has been a grass-roots movement – not one born of precepts brought down from above. It has been a response of practical compassion often rooted in a Christian worldview that refuses to accept that in the market the only categories are winners and losers. The concept of fair trade is worked out as trading organisations work with the poor producers to address what they need and want. It is a grass-roots approach to express a concern that those in the Two Thirds World gain from participation in trade rather than be subject to it.

Judith Sugden argues that the point of fair trade is that [poor] producers' [legitimate and just] interests are met. An approach that addresses producer interests and needs from the grass-roots out of a concern for social justice has extremely positive results in terms of poverty alleviation, social development and extending the producer interests into the mainstream.[6]

Poor producers need markets. Fair trade organisations have provided a niche market, and placed a premium on products as the volume of fairly traded goods is too small to benefit from economies of scale. But poor producers need help in accessing the mainstream international market within a framework which ensures they are not exploited. They are not there just to challenge consumers' consciences. The increase in the fair trade movement has encouraged many poor producers whose primary need is access to the market. Poor producer interests can be met by enabling them to enter the international market through business development, credit schemes, labelling and the development of ethical trading. This goes beyond the role of Alternative Trading Organisations.

What ATOs can achieve is limited. In 1990 the estimated annual earnings of ATOs were 250 million pounds; the income of Tate and Lyle, one international trader in sugar, was 3,432 million pounds. But 'by acting as prototypes for the new initiatives, [ATOs] demonstrate to other trading companies that fair trade principles can be applied to all aspects of the market and are viable within it.'[7] The activities of ATOs can have an influence out of all proportion to their size. Traidcraft has provided considerable input to the Labour Party's policy on the role of business in international development, and to the British Government's White Paper on International Development. But that input depends on it putting those principles to the test in its own business.

Traidcraft has grown as a grass-roots prophetic movement seeking justice, offering prototypes for new initiatives in trading and business relationships. This follows the pattern of Christian involvement in medicine and education. Christians were often the first to begin schools and hospitals and are often still the first to do so in poor and remote areas. Other people of good will saw the contribution of their work. In time other organisations and governments themselves took on the responsibility of providing universal access to education and health. The response of Christians has been twofold: first, to take their own place in the new national institutions; second, to pioneer new areas. Thus in the UK Health Service, Christians pioneered the Hospice Movement which is now gaining similar wide acceptance.

How do the activities of Traidcraft express some of these biblical patterns today?

First, *Traidcraft's work in seeking justice through trade is a frontier of the Kingdom with the current economic order.* What would the world economic order look like if the Kingdom of God came tomorrow morning? There would be justice in exchange and trade. If God's final Kingdom of peace and righteousness will be marked by justice and that Kingdom has entered the world already in Jesus, then we are called to show signs of the Kingdom at the frontiers of rebellious human society. Working for justice through trade demonstrates what the Kingdom looks like when it encounters the injustice of the world economic trading systems. This signpost points in turn to Jesus Christ, whose resurrection assures us that this Kingdom will one day finally triumph.

Secondly, *Traidcraft activities act as a kind of parable.* If we were to knock on people's front doors and explain that the poverty of the poor was intimately linked with them, many would probably give us no more than a ten second hearing. A Traidcraft stall and Traidcraft goods draw people in rather like a parable. They come, perhaps out of a sense of compassion for those who suffer. We encourage them to purchase goods made in the Two-Thirds World, and with the educational backup suggest that it is not so much compassion for those who suffer as justice for those who are wronged. One Fair Trader told me how someone had come to her stall in church one day with friends and commented, 'I wouldn't have those apricots if I were you, they have been touched by brown hands.' An embarrassed silence fell. It was clear to everyone, and finally to the shopper herself, that she had passed a judgement on herself. Traidcraft's parabolic ministry moves people one step forward. They can never be the same again.

Thirdly, *Traidcraft is an event with an explanation.* The event is the event of a Traidcraft sale. The explanation is why we should purchase goods from the Two-Thirds World, often at a higher price than in the supermarkets. The explanation is about justice and fairness – about why buy from such groups and communities. The ultimate answer is because the reality of the universe is shown in Jesus who shows that the Lord of the world is a Lord of justice and mercy whose will is that all have the opportunity to manage the earth.

Fourthly, *Traidcraft opens up a relationship between the poor and the non-poor.* Many analyses of poverty and prescriptions for dealing with it set the poor in conflict with the non-poor. In Christian terms it is the work of evil (the principalities and powers) to create division out of difference, whether in race, gender, class or material resources. The work of Jesus Christ is to break down the barriers between separated and hostile groups. This is the clear teaching of Ephesians 2–3. The dwelling place of the Holy Spirit is a community where such barriers have been broken. Jesus spoke of the destructive power of Mammon in people's lives. It is a rival divinity to God, which leads people to get their priorities wrong, and prevents them from entering God's Kingdom where they would find fulfilment of their humanity. It blinds people to the needs of others. To enter the Kingdom people need to renounce wealth (Mk. 10:27); love for riches is a major obstacle to spiritual growth (Mk. 4:19), and fields, oxen and marriage arrangements lead people to refuse God's invitation. The cross made community between hostile groups possible. So the reaction of biblical Christians to those different from themselves should be to seek partnership. Vinay Samuel points out that

> Because the prime categories [are] those saved by Christ and those as yet unsaved, the biblical Christian does not think of rich and poor as the primary divisions or categories. The understanding the poor has of the rich is not of a powerful oppressor, but of a person. The evangelical never feels powerless against the rich. He or she still feels he or she has the gospel to share. The slum dweller may lack much, but has the priceless treasure of Christ, the hope of glory. Therefore the poor need never accept the rich as people who cannot change. They can confidently, not arrogantly, share something with the rich that the rich need.[8]

In the process of this sharing the rich also can develop a new basis for their identity – the grace of God in Christ. In the parable of the rich fool, Jesus teaches that riches blind people to the Kingdom of God because rich people tend to seek their identity and security in wealth. That approach leads to endless anxiety and worry. Jesus encourages people to seek their security in the Kingdom of God, in the care of the heavenly Father who provides for the birds and the flowers. God will provide the basic necessities of life for his subjects. So they have no need to use up their energy worrying about their future, persecution or death. Instead, free of self-concern they can give their attention to living by the standards of God's Kingdom for just relationships. Since God will provide their necessities, members of the Kingdom can give to the poor.

Giving to the poor is saving up treasure in heaven (Lk. 12:33) and enables trust in God to be expressed. Jesus points out that people are to seek first the Kingdom of God and everything else will be added to them. Once people seek their security in the right place, they are freed from pouring their resources into the bottomless pit of seeking security in riches. They are then free to give alms to the poor.

People are not free to help the poor because they believe they need all their wealth to ensure their own security. The sin of the man who planned bigger barns is similar to the sin of the man who hid his talent in the ground. (Matt. 26: 14–30). Their strategy was based on self-centred fear. The sin for which 'bigger barns' is condemned is not his concern for material things. Jesus affirms that God knows we need food and clothes. The rich fool did not care for the poor because he was anxious to ensure that he had bigger barns in which to store all his goods so that he could enjoy life. If such a person is counselled to share with the poor, the real hurdle he/she must overcome is anxiety about their security. Jesus equates giving alms to the poor with providing treasure in heaven. Paul does the same in 1 Timothy 6: 7–10. Alms to the poor was the dominant form of social relief in Jesus' time. Thus those who invest their time and their resources in activity which benefits the poorest, who are showing compassion in a world which only thinks of winners and losers, where people are in slavery to greed or fear, according to Jesus, will reap treasure in heaven. Treasure in heaven is using resources to enable the poor to have their full place in society. Earthly treasures are of use in the Kingdom.

This is good news for the rich. Jesus sets them free from rebelling against God by seeking security in their wealth; this expresses no trust in God because riches are being laid up for the self. People then cannot and do not give money or time to the needs of the poor because they need everything to bolster their own need for security which can never be satisfied. Jesus sets people free to devote their attention and wealth to the concerns of God's Kingdom, God's right relationships, and especially the poor. This new basis for their identity and security as good news to the rich derives in part from the meaning of the good news to the poor which gives the poor a new identity. Rich and poor experience this new identity together because both have been accepted in grace at the cross of Christ. When this understanding is lacking, a process sets in of blaming and fearing others and ignoring the sins in their own communities which contribute to the problem.

Christ's atoning death needs to be central as the basis of forgiveness. God has forgiven us all an unpayable debt so that we may forgive the debts we owe one another. If a sense of Christ's death is not present, people cannot easily let go of the sense of the wrongs they have suffered or that they have been party to inflicting on others. Victims continuously present themselves as victims. They take on an heroic, even Messianic role. A competition emerges to demonstrate that one particular group is undergoing the worst suffering. The guilty have continually to express their guilt and atone for it by keeping silent or by a self-righteous posturing on behalf of the oppressed.

Christian organisations engaged in ministry with the poor can be signs of the new identity that God gives the poor and the rich as they serve as partners that express the new sharing in one community between people divided by one of the major causes of division in society – Mammon. Organisations such as Traidcraft provide a mechanism by which those with resources can use them to assist the poor to fulfil their human potential and calling to be stewards. Surveys of purchasers of Traidcraft products show them to be predominantly located among middle-class people, and within England in the Southern and Eastern half of the country. They can afford the premium price of fair trade products. The process links such people in a partnership that gives the poor producers a market, and enables people who by any global standard are 'rich' to enter into a trading relationship which questions many of the assumptions of their own culture.

WHY A CHRISTIAN ORGANISATION?

Assisting poor people to fulfil their calling to be stewards, through a mechanism of trade conducted in accord with principles of justice, in a process that provides a link between poor and non-poor and loans to poor people, depends on a particular view of humanity. This view sees human beings as more than objects of charity; human relations as defined by more than economics; the division between human communities brought by Mammon as an evil power that holds people in its grip which can only be fully addressed by the cross of Christ that overcomes such evil and such divisions; human rights as applicable to the community relationships of people; and the differences between people and groups as occasions for working in partnership rather than divisions to be overcome through conflict.

Many beyond the Christian community share such a view. This happens because on a Christian view the one place where we see evil overcome in the world is the cross of Christ. Therefore any activity or action that expresses the victory of good over evil, and takes forward the forces of life over against the forces of darkness, is ultimately attributable to Christ's victory over evil on the cross. Those who work to forward the well-being of humanity without consciously acknowledging the source or goal of life are nevertheless able to make their contribution because of what the cross of Christ has achieved. The witness of Christian partnership to them is to point to the source, empowerment and goal of such a process which more often than not will become a relevant issue somewhere along the line.

But some will question the basis for such a view of humanity. It is here that the inextricable link between religion and assisting poor people is seen.

First, *a religious view of the world is inevitably involved when discussing the nature and identity of human beings.* For example, as Christians we believe that the economic condition of poor people does not define who they really are. The Bible presents them as beloved creatures of God called to steward his creation and called to be members of his Kingdom, whatever their economic condition. The Bible's call to Christian disciples is to be partners in releasing them to address their poverty with dignity; the dignity that knows that they are not defined by their circumstances; that they can hope for a better future for them and their families; that they can express trust and honour and integrity in their business dealings; to offer them the opportunity to compete in the market place on fair terms with dignity; to value themselves and their products.

The Christian gospel brings that dignity to people. When the orders finish, when the market changes, when the NGO, the suitcase people as they are known, are gone, people's dignity does not disappear when it is founded on the knowledge that they are supremely valuable to God. Dignity is rooted finally not in trade but in God's grace. His grace may use trade and our work as a channel to reinforce and express what he does, but unless people find their ultimate dignity in the dignity God gives them, they are short changed yet again.

Secondly, the world is continually re-learning, often at great cost, *the link between religion and morality.* In September 1998 with colleagues from around the world, I visited Vukovar, the Croatian city on the borders of Serbia. Vukovar had been beseiged and taken by Serbian forces during the civil war. It was handed back to Croatia in January 1998. It had been devastated. 12,000 of its population of 60,000 had been killed. In a powerful speech, the President of the District spoke of her community's pledge to reshape their education system. She said they had been brought to this pass through 70 years of a system that divorced religion and morality. As a result people had neither respected ties of family nor humanity in the awful slaughter. They were therefore committed to raising the next generation to understand the religious roots of human morality. Vinay Samuel has pointed out that the Christian faith and the church have been marginalised in social action in Europe since the Enlightenment which insisted that religion is not a source of human development. As a result, governments and secular relief agencies suggest that humanism is the best framework for human social development. Vukovar indicates that what is needed is to recover a moral vision for society rooted in religious conviction. This has been recognised by the World Bank which has recently concluded an agreement with the churches in Africa to work in partnership to alleviate poverty. The World Bank recognised that there is a need for a moral vision to undergird sustainable development, and that the churches represent a long term presence among the poor precisely because of their moral vision rooted in their religious convictions.

Thirdly, *most poor people in the world are religious and relate their situation in some way to religion.* They are often more open to work with and trust people who make a religious commitment than those of whose commitments they are unsure. Research by the World Bank, among 60,000 poor people worldwide published as *Voices of the Poor* (2000), indicates that, after their own organisations, poor people place most trust in religious organisations to help them.

Fourthly, *a Christian approach to assisting poor people should not act in a form of practical welfarism,* as though economics dictates everything in life. On the contrary, those working in development have time and again discovered that a fundamental issue for poor people is who they are. Their religious societies tell them they are defiled and cursed; economic comparisons tell them they are losers. The Christian gospel tells them that they are created as stewards of God and called to be his children through grace, despite their supposed demerits. The greatest evidence for this is the cross of Christ which brings the good news that victory over all opposing and evil powers has been won. Part of the culture of poor people which enables them to cope psychologically with the harshness of their existence is that it is their fate that they are paying a price for somebody's action somewhere. In religious terms it may be a price for the past sins of their family; or in anticipation of future blessedness. In secular terms it may be the price for past structural oppression, or in anticipation of national economic recovery. This reinforces in the poor a sense of victimisation at the hands of forces they cannot control. They attribute to these forces enormous power before which they are helpless. Thus fate also stifles creativity and responsibility. This false consciousness is an expression of sin and death that destroys God's purpose for life.

The atonement announces that the price is already paid for the past and that the price of the future is secured. This releases in people a new sense of identity. They are somebody. By grace they are not damnable and useless people. They are called to be sons and daughters of God; to be friends of Jesus; to be inheritors of the promises of God; and in the church, the bride of Christ. As his creation they are called to have dominion over the earth and are accountable to him. As his children they are restored to this position despite their supposed and real demerits, because of the cross. Indwelt by God's Spirit, they have access to the power of God through prayer, to the armory of God against evil, and to the resources of God which are far more than material. This is true empowerment.

The forces of the global market economy marginalise religion. For the wealthy of the world to deny poor people not only access to economic resources but also to deny the reality of the world of religion which gives an alternative basis for identity to that which is defined by the rich is a double deprivation. Christian involvement to assist poor people may not always be religious in expression; but it is necessarily religious in foundation as this is a powerful alternative basis from which to challenge the definitions and frameworks the wealthy put on the world. These definitions and frameworks are constantly changing. A Christian response to them needs to be constantly updated. Over the last fifty years the predominant western Christian response to poverty has moved, where it has gone beyond indifference, from provision of welfare, to involvement in nation building, to community awareness building and education, to trade and micro-credit enterprise. We cannot assume we have reached the final and sufficient solution. There will be new challenges and new responses. We are already seeing ideas of fair trade and small scale business development being taken up by supermarket chains (B&Q) and world organisations (the World Bank). In this we rejoice. But in the process they will be open to misuse and abuse. A Christian organisation must also constantly review its own analysis of problems and advocacy of solutions in the light of God's revealed will in scripture. It must also recognise that Christian values must be rooted in and resourced by a living relation to Jesus Christ. The traditions of humanitarianism, however worthy, will not be adequate on their own.

Thus Christian faith-based organisations have an important place in the field of assistance to the poor. This is not just because the poor need to hear the gospel. The poor need an approach to dealing with the problems of poverty and enabling them to obtain true humanity which constantly seeks to maintain the quality of God's will for human beings; an approach which addresses the oppressive structures of world trade; which seeks to enable poor people to develop their own entrepreneurial skills; which believes them to be worthy of credit and to receive loans; which sees a role for the non-poor in addressing their situation; which enables them to build their families and their communities; which sees the importance of fair wages and reward; which provides space for compassionate action; which speaks to governments about the poor of the earth; which works for benefits to communities; and which addresses the divisions between people caused by Mammon. All these components are rooted in a biblical understanding of human beings as created persons in community, called to be stewards in a world where evil has been overcome in the cross of Christ.

TRAIDCRAFT AND THE CHURCHES

Traidcraft is a Christian Development Business and Agency. It is not a church. But Christian Development Organisations are an expression of the churches' engagement with society. Vinay Samuel points out that they are the mission presence of the church, a mission community of the church.[9] This does two things. It prevents development agencies becoming utterly secular in reducing the totality of development to social and economic factors. A community cannot be built with reference to finance and economics alone. Economic sustainability depends on vision. If people have a vision they will find the economics. The churches are bearers of a moral vision. Is it possible to build a community without a vital church presence, with a commitment to the disabled and the poor?

This focus also enables Christian Development agencies to do what they can do and to maintain their particularity as development organisations rather than become civil society institutions. It is important to limit the work of development agencies to what they are called to do; to prevent them pouring resources into what they cannot do; to keep to their task of bringing effective development to local communities. The most effective projects have been where the local community is capacitated by the church. Development Agencies should work in partnership with those who prevent them becoming everything in the community they serve. Development Agencies do not want to be part of the local community forever. They must be involved in programmes that are sustainable without their presence. So the development agencies need the churches to provide communities with a moral vision and a civil society framework. The churches need development agencies as expressions of the church so that the churches do not need to become development agencies.

That is why it is important that Traidcraft sees the church as a major partner. The churches are an important partner in the UK, as a source of shareholders, fair traders and consumers. Such people support Traidcraft because it transmits their honour and valuing of poor people and their passion to partner them. Church people trust Traidcraft to treat people in trade as they would wish as Christians to treat them. Traidcraft helps us all understand the gospel as it takes concrete expression in fair trade with dignity for poor people.

The church is also an important partner in producer countries. Because it is the gospel which gives poor people the dignity that at root changes their lives, it is the gospel that constrains the church to be with and among the poor. In some African countries NGO's reach 7% of the poor at most. The church reaches 90% of them. The contribution which the Christian community makes to serving the poor in poor countries is out of all proportion to their size or resources. They need and deserve to know about the partnership that Traidcraft offers the poor.

Christian fair trade organisations can show the frontier of the Kingdom of God with the current economic order; enable people to become stewards of creation; can be a parable that changes people one step at a time, but irrevocably; and an event that can give opportunity for an explanation that is rooted in why we believe justice is so fundamental and why we believe that action for justice is not in vain.

BIBLIOGRAPHY

Fair Trade

Adams, Richard, *Who Profits? A Revealing Case Study in Successful Trading with Developing Countries* (Oxford: Lion, 1989).

Adams, Richard, Carruthers, Jane and Fisher, Charlie, *Shopping for a Better World: A Quick and Easy Guide to Socially Responsible Shopping* (London: Kogan Page, 1991).

Adams, Richard, Wells, Phil and Webb, Iris, *For a Better World: A Social Action Guide for Christians* (Oxford: Lynx, 1994).

Barratt Brown, Michael, *Fair Trade: Reform and Realities in the International Trading System* (London: Zed Books, 1993).

Burns, Sara, *Fair Trade: A Rough Guide for Business* (London: TWIN, 1996).

Cho, George, *Trade and Global Interdependence* (London: Routledge, 1995).

Coote, Belinda, *The Trade Trap: Poverty and the Global Commodity Markets* (Oxford: Oxfam, 1992).

Davenport, M. and Page, S., *World Trade Reform: Do Developing Countries Win or Lose?* (London: Overseas Development Institute, 1994).

Dobson, Andrew, *Green Political Thought* (London: Routledge, 1995).

European Fair Trade Association, *Fair Trade Yearbook* (Maastricht: European Fair Trade Association, 1995).

Ekins, Paul, *A New World Order: Grass Roots Movements for Social Change* (London: Routledge, 1992).

Goldsmith, James, *The Response: Gatt and Global Free Trade* (London: Macmillan, 1995).

Madden, Peter, *A Raw Deal: Trade and the World's Poor* (London: Christian Aid, 1992).

Madeley, John, *Trade and the Poor: The Impact of International Trade on Developing Countries* (London: Intermediate Technology Publications, 1992).

Overseas Development Administration, 'Microfinance is now big Business', Internet article http://www.oneworld.org/oda/publications/bod47/business.html

Page, S., *How Developing Countries Trade* (London, Routledge, 1994).

Vallely, Paul, *Promised Lands: Stories of Power and Poverty in the Third World* (London: Fount and Christian Aid, 1992).

Christian Mission and the Poor

Belshaw, Deryke; Calderisi, Robert and Sugden, Chris, *Faith in Development: Possibilities for Partnership between the World Bank and the Churches of Africa* (Oxford: Regnum, and Washington: World Bank, 2001).

Bussau, David, *Reflections on Christian Microenterprise Development* (Oxford: Opportunity International, 1999).

Bussau, David and Samuel, Vinay, *How then should we lend? A Biblical Validation of Microenterprise Development* (Oxford: Opportunity International, 1999).

Costas, Orlando, *Liberating News* (Grand Rapids: Eerdmans 1989).

de Santa Ana, Julio, *Good News to the Poor* (Geneva: WCC, 1977).

Fung, Raymond, 'Good News to the Poor – a case for a missionary movement' in *Your Kingdom Come* (Geneva: WCC, 1980).

Hall, Douglas, *The Steward – A Biblical Symbol Come of Age* (New York: Friendship Press, 1982).

Houston, Tom, 'Good News for the Poor', in *Transformation* January 1990, Vol. 7, No. 1.

Mason, John, 'Biblical Teaching and Assisting the Poor' in *Transformation,* April 1987, Vol. 4 No. 2.

Petersen, Douglas, *Not by Might nor by Power* (Oxford: Regnum, 1996).

Samuel, Vinay and Colleen, 'Rebuilding Families – a Priority for Wholistic Mission' in *Transformation* July 1993, Vol. 9 No. 3.

Samuel,Vinay and Sugden, Chris, *Evangelism and the Poor* (Exeter: Paternoster, 1983) pp. 37–106.

Samuel, Vinay and Sugden Chris, *Mission as Transformation* (Oxford: Regnum, 2000).

Sarracco, Norberto, 'The Liberating Options of Jesus' in *Sharing Jesus in the Two Thirds World*, edited by Vinay Samuel and Chris Sugden (Grand Rapids: Eerdmans, 1986).

Schlossberg, Herbert, Samuel, Vinay and Sider, Ronald J., *Christianity and Economics in the Post-Cold War Era* (Grand Rapids: Eerdmans, 1994).

Sider, Ronald J., *Rich Christians in an Age of Hunger* (London: Hodder and Stoughton, 1978).

Sider, Ronald J., *Evangelism and Social Action* (London: Hodder and Stoughton, 1993), Appendix 'Is Social Justice Part of Salvation?'.

Sider, Ronald J., *Cup of Water, Bread of Life* (Grand Rapids: Zondervan, 1994).

Sugden, Chris, 'Poverty' in *New Dictionary of Theology*, edited by S.B. Ferguson and D.F. Wright, (Leicester: Inter Varsity Press,

1988).

Sugden, Chris 'What is Good about Good News to the Poor?', in *AD 2000 and Beyond – A Mission Agenda*, edited by Vinay Samuel and Chris Sugden (Oxford: Regnum, 1991).

Sugden, Chris and Barclay, Oliver *Kingdom and Creation in Social Ethics* (Cambridge: Grove Booklets, 1990).

Sugden, Chris *Fair Trade as Christian Mission* (Cambridge: Grove Books, 1999).

Sugden, Chris *Seeking The Asian Face of Jesus* (Oxford: Regnum, 1997).

Sugden, Chris, 'Jesus Christ, Saviour and Liberator', in *Sharing Good News with the Poor*, edited by Bruce Nicholls and Beulah Wood (Carlisle: Paternoster, 1996).

'Charity which gives nothing away' in *Christian Action Journal*, Autumn 1993.

'Children at Risk', in *Transformation,* April 1997, Vol. 14 No. 2.

'Christian Faith and Economics Revisited 2: A New Partnership for Poverty Alleviation in Africa', *Transformation*, October 2000, Vol. 17 No. 4.

'A Christian Response to Disability' in *Transformation,* October 1998, Vol. 15 No. 4.

'Oxford Declaration on Christian Faith and Economics' in *Transformation*, April 1990, Vol. 7 No. 2.

NOTES

1   This material is a revised and updated form of material published by the author as *Fair Trade as Christian Mission* (Cambridge: Grove Books, 1999), which includes a more extended discussion of the nature of Fair Trade.

2   *Christian Witness to the Urban Poor* published by the Lausanne Committee for World Evangelisation from their consultation in Thailand in 1980; reproduced in *Evangelism and the Poor* edited by Vinay Samuel and Chris Sugden (Exeter: Paternoster, 1982), pp. 46–47.

3   Report of the Social Concern Track of Lausanne II at Manila, June 1989, published in *Transformation* July 1990, Vol. 7 No. 3 p. 2. Also in 'What is Good about Good News to the Poor?' in *AD 2000 and Beyond – A Mission Agenda* edited by Vinay Samuel and Chris Sugden (Oxford: Regnum, 1991), p. 57.

4   John Mason, 'Assistance Programmes in the Bible, *Transformation* April 1987, Vol. 4 No. 2 pp. 3–5.

5   'Is there a fair trade model that can be extended to International Trade at a Macro-Level?' by Judith Sugden (unpublished Durham University, BA Dissertation in Combined Studies for Social Sciences, 1997), p. 66.

6   Judith Sugden, *op.cit.*, pp. 71–72.

7   Judith Sugden, *op.cit.*, p. 70.

8   Vinay Samuel quoted in Chris Sugden 'Jesus Christ, Saviour and Liberator', in B.J. Nicholls and B.R. Wood (eds.) *Sharing Good News with the Poor* (Carlisle, Paternoster 1996), p.90.

9   Vinay Samuel, 'The Relation between Development Agencies, Christian Development Societies and the Church', unpublished paper, Network for Anglicans in Mission and Evangelism Resources for the Churches, Oxford, May 2000.

Chapter Two

Renewing the Market Place[1]

Peter Johnson

INTRODUCTION

Market activity is embedded in all of our lives. We buy goods and services, we lend and we borrow; and many of us supply labour services for which we are paid. If we are owners of a business, we purchase a wide variety of services and supplies, transform them into output, and seek to sell that output in the market place. Every day, millions of transactions, varying enormously in value and complexity, are completed. This chapter explores some of the issues and challenges that these market activities generate for Christian discipleship. The next section considers some of the pluses and minuses of market activity. The third section then looks at the nature of the market in order to highlight some relevant issues for market participation. The fourth section outlines a number of underlying principles for such participation. The final section offers some concluding reflections.

SOME PLUSES AND MINUSES

A BASIC FREEDOM

Much of the following discussion on the benefits of markets focuses on the economic results of market activities. As Sen (1999, p. 6) has recently pointed out, however, it is important to recognise that "the freedom of exchange and transactions [implied by markets] is itself part and parcel of the basic liberties that people have reason to value.' Sen continues (the italics are his):

> To be *generically against* markets would be almost as odd as
> being generically against conversations between people.... The
> freedom to exchange words, or good, or gifts does not need
> defensive justification in terms of their favourable but distant
> effects; they are part of the way human beings in society live and
> interact with each other (unless stopped by regulation or fiat).

It is important to bear Sen's point in mind in the debate about
the pros and cons of market activities.

THE MARKET'S CO-ORDINATING ROLE

The essential economic function of the market system is to co-
ordinate economic activity. This co-ordination function is a
massive operation. Even the humblest items that come into our
possession – the tea bag, the pencil, the glass of water – are only
there because of a highly complex chain of interrelated market
transactions, which in some cases stretch around the globe. The
evidence of this co-ordination confronts us every day of our
lives. For example, each car that passes us on the road is a testimony to the success of a market co-ordination process, which
brings together thousands of components in one engineering
construction. Its servicing, the provision of petrol, oil and water
and the spare parts that are necessary to keep it on the road provide further evidence of this process. And the occupants of the
car may themselves be playing a part in yet another string of
transactions. They may for example be going to a business
meeting, or be travelling engineers or sales people or mobile
hairdressers.

Of course we may want to point out that not all cars are as
good a witness to the success of the co-ordination process as
others, but it would be difficult to deny the immensity of the
market co-ordination task that they represent. The way in which
thousands of different contributions are co-ordinated within a
market system is in many ways quite remarkable, and is a tribute to human creativity. Perhaps we should be more explicitly
thankful for this than we are: signs of God's providence may be
seen in the market co-ordination process.

For most of the time, the co-ordination provided by the

market proceeds untrumpeted and without fuss, and we take it for granted. Our purchase of a loaf in the supermarket for example, rarely causes us to pause to think of the complex chain of activity and contracts that makes that purchase possible. It is only when things go wrong that we start investigating the process. The fact that we mostly take the co-ordination process for granted – notwithstanding the stimulus for further debate on the topic that comes from the huge literature on the interface between Christian belief (in its various brands) and markets[2] – carries the danger that we will miss the challenges that it raises for our behaviour.

OUTPUT-ENHANCING EFFECTS OF A MARKET SYSTEM

Why go to all this trouble of co-ordinating economic activity? Is it all really necessary? For an insight into why the need for co-ordination arises, it is necessary to look at the role of specialisation in production. Adam Smith (1776) was the first to detail the benefits of specialisation in his Wealth of Nations. He used the 'very trifling' example of pin-making (1776, vol. I, pp. 8–9). He argued that if ten men specialised on particular tasks in the pin-making production line, they could make upwards of 48,000 pins a day, but that if each man worked on his own, doing all of the component tasks himself, 20 pins per person would be an absolute maximum (he might be unable to make even one). The same principle can be applied generally: within limits (of which Adam Smith was himself only too aware: 1776, vol. II, p. 302), specialisation increases the amount that can be produced from a given set of inputs.

Now there may be some increases in goods and services which we might judge to be undesirable, either because they seem excessive, or because of the characteristics of the output, but an enhancement in overall material well-being has many potentially positive aspects to it. It can be harnessed for the alleviation of poverty and for the enhancement of opportunities for human enjoyment, development and choice. It is worth noting, too, that material prosperity is sometimes seen in the Old Testament as a token of God's kindness and something for which to be thankful: for example, references are made to overflowing barns as a sign of blessing (Ps. 144: 12–15).

The critical point for us to note from all this is that the gains from specialisation can only be obtained if there is some mechanism for redistributing output. A pin factory employee cannot eat or wear pins. It is here that the market system has obvious relevance: it provides a way of enabling people to enjoy the benefits of specialisation. The presence of a medium of exchange – money – means that interdependence is not limited only to cases where barter is possible. Thus it is possible to economise on agreement (which is often costly) since there is no requirement for a double coincidence of wants.[3] Christian teaching has rightly focused on the downside of money, but this should not blind us to its facilitating role in exchange.

The market's role as a facilitator of exchange between specialists, and hence of higher material well-being, points to two more fundamental benefits. First, the market may be seen as enhancing our sense of interdependence, of our need for one another, of community, of being members one of another.[4] We are able, through our participation in the market, to contribute to the good of others. The notion of the dovetailing of different specialist contributions is not unfamiliar to readers of the scriptures. Two (rather different) examples are the specialisation of skills in the building of the tabernacle (Ex. 35–36) and specialisation of spiritual gifts within the church, the body of believers (1 Cor. 12).

The second benefit of a more fundamental kind is that while specialisation emphasises our interrelatedness, it also, at the same time, underlines our individuality and specialness. It may be helpful to think again of the analogy of the body of Christ. Although our dependence as Christians on one another is a key lesson from 1 Corinthians 12, it is not the only one. The image of the separate parts of the body also highlights the distinctive, special role of each individual.

THE SIGNALLING ROLE OF MARKETS

Alongside their role as fora for exchanging the fruits of specialisation, markets also provide signals – albeit imperfect ones – about shortages and excess supply. In this way they encourage adjustment in the patterns of demand and supply as technological conditions and customer preferences change. They may also provide direct encouragement for innovative activity by pointing to potential opportunities for new developments, and providing a mechanism for obtaining a return on such developments.

SOME LESS ATTRACTIVE ASPECTS

There are a number of characteristics of the private market system that are unattractive from a Christian perspective. Two may be mentioned here. The first is that we can only participate if we have something to offer that someone else wants. Essentially a market is the exchange of property rights, whether those rights are an individual's financial resources, labour, intellect and skills, or in other inputs or possessions. Market prices and quantities will thus reflect the distribution of property rights. Shortages and excess supply are only interpretable in the context of this distribution. 'Voting power' on the demand side of the market place, determined principally by income, will often be an apparent accident of birth. It may even be the result of theft by some past generation. If individuals have nothing to offer, then they have no role in the market place. It is interesting to note in this context that safeguards against the concentration of wealth were built into Jewish law, for example, through the Year of Jubilee (Lev. 25:8–9). It is interesting too that within tribes, the initial allocation of land in Canaan was by lots, and apparently on an equal shares basis (Num. 33:54).

The second source of uneasiness about the market arises because the main driving force behind market operations is typically self-interest. The desire to get the best bargain possible underpins the market system. Adam Smith again (1776, vol. I, p. 13): 'It is not from the benevolence of the butcher, the brewer, or the baker that we expect our dinner, but from their regard to their own interest.' Both the buyer and the seller give as little as he/she can get away with. Both often seek to drive the other down. As Proverbs 20:14 (*Good News Bible*) says, 'The customer always complains that the price is too high....'

Now within limits, self-interest may be seen as God-given.

Harries has pointed out (1992, p. 91) that without some level of self-interest, we would not survive. And there are some passages of scripture that suggest that a basic caring for self is legitimate and embodied in our psyche anyway.

This justification of self-interest is clearly a limited one. However, Adam Smith pointed to an altogether wider justification for self-interest which has been analysed by countless generations of economics students. He argued that the outcome of the operation of a competitive market system – of 'the invisible hand'[5] – is the best for society as a whole. By seeking individual self-interest, the best outcome for society is achieved. Trade only occurs because *both* parties benefit, and resources move to the activities that have the highest values. *Competitive* markets are, however, an essential prerequisite for the social welfare enhancing role of the market. It has long been acknowledged that all kinds of distortion may arise from collusion and the exercise of market dominance.

There is another aspect of self-interest that may have destructive effects, even in competitive markets. It arises because market players, motivated solely by their own interests, will take maximum advantage of situations where they can obtain resources, or goods and services without any contractual requirement to pay for them, either in part or in full. A firm may, for example, utilise a production process that pollutes the atmosphere without paying the cost of so doing. Such negative 'externalities' arise because property rights – in this case, in clean air – are absent, or are not well defined, or are not enforced. The existence of *positive* externalities – where the decision-maker may not receive all the *benefits* resulting from his or her decision – also creates distortions in market outcomes, since the resources likely to be attracted into activities where such externalities are present is likely to be lower than would be justified by the total return obtainable.

Some key plus and minus characteristics of the market have been briefly examined. What are we, as Christians, to make of it all? The evidence of our own eyes suggests that all is not well. We *observe* awful poverty and human degradation, and some enormous disparities in wealth and income. We *observe* high levels of unemployment in some countries and areas, and all the misery that entails. We *observe* whole communities having their livelihood taken from them as businesses shut down. While the causes of this suffering are complex, and extend beyond the effects of market processes, these processes nevertheless play an often crucial role. We also see markets throwing up much that, on almost any criteria, is cheap, nasty and sordid, and which appeals to human greed.

How should we respond to these challenges? The problems markets throw up do not of themselves justify the wholesale jettisoning of the market system. *When viewed against the alternatives*, the market system has much to commend it as the preferred option. As Boulding says: 'The case for the market is certainly the moral and economic inadequacy of the alternatives' (in Block, et al., eds.,1985, p. 254).[6] The fact that there are major problems with this system, does not mean that an alternative system would be better. A key challenge therefore for Christians is: how can the current system be improved? To tackle this question it is helpful to return to first principles, and to start with the question of what a market is.

WHAT IS A MARKET?

A market is simply the arena in which voluntary exchange between buyers and sellers takes place. It may involve a shop, a travel agency, a factory, the mail order catalogue, a web site, and so on. Such exchange may involve barter, where goods and/or services are exchanged, or, more commonly in the UK, it may occur when one of the parties parts with money in return for goods and/or services. The exchange may involve the full transfer of ownership, or a hire arrangement. Each exchange involves an explicit or implicit contract.

Now there are a number of features of this system that should be noted. Perhaps the most important for our purposes is that the market may be seen simply as the location for human action. Seen in this way, the market has no values. *It is the human actors who enter the forum for the purposes of trading that have the values*. It is easy to lose sight of this characteristic and the challenges it presents to us as Christians.

A sense of 'distance' between market activities and the

values of the participants is created by the perception that we do not see ourselves as exercising any influence over market activity. Even if we wanted to exercise some influence, we see ourselves as unable to do so. 'The market' and 'market forces' have increasingly been seen as impersonal influences which we simply have to accept, much as we might have to accept the weather or our metabolism. We are frequently told that 'the market' has reacted positively or negatively to a particular event or policy, as if no one is involved. Judgements are attributed to the 'market', which is said to approve or disapprove of a particular development. In this way, no individual, or group of individuals ever has to take – nor can they take – any kind of moral responsibility for market forces. In this way, markets grant a spurious kind of moral absolution. Sadly, economists have unintentionally reinforced this no-one-is-responsible view of markets by the way in which they have approached the analysis of competitive market activity, where individual buyers and sellers are seen as having no power to influence market forces.

There is of course a sense in which it is true that no one person can affect a market's behaviour. There is precious little that an individual buyer or seller can do to affect the world price of wheat, or the share price of ICI. But it is important to remember that markets only exist because of the participation, either directly or indirectly, through institutions, of men and women in them. This participation inevitably involves decisions, attitudes and motivations. It is not the 'market' that is greedy, or bent solely on selfish commercial gain, but the people who participate in its operation. The Christian faith therefore has direct relevance to what is happening in markets. We cannot excuse ourselves from the moral responsibility of market participation simply on the grounds that there are millions of individuals playing in the same game, with no one individual having a noticeable effect.

The fact that no one individual can influence market activity in any significant way may not simply generate a sense of helplessness; it may sometimes be used to *justify* an action. We may, for example, argue that market forces mean that we are required to act in a particular way. This in turn raises important ethical issues.

Secondly, the fact that exchange may be entered into voluntarily does not necessarily mean that the contracting parties are equally matched in terms of their contracting position. They may differ in a number of ways. For example, they may differ in the amount of relevant information that they possess. This problem of 'asymmetric information' between contracting parties, which has generated a vast economic literature, is familiar to most of us. The tour operator may know that not far from the hotel that the tourist has booked, there is a noisy building site. The brochure makes no reference to this activity in its description of the hotel, although the small print, that only the most assiduous customer reads, absolves the operator of any responsibility for any inconvenience caused by building work.

The classic example of asymmetric information is found in the second-hand car market. The buyer with little technical knowledge cannot easily judge whether the car is in good mechanical order. The owner on the other hand may know the car intimately, or may have better knowledge to make a technical judgement.

Now there may of course sometimes be ways round this asymmetry. The tourist may become a member of a consumer group that evaluates different tour operators. The car buyer may employ someone who is better qualified to evaluate the car for him, or may purchase technical, evaluative reports. However, it may not always be possible to purchase such protection. There may, for example, be no easy way of providing a pre-purchase evaluation. A meal in a newly opened restaurant can only be evaluated by buying it. One might not even know what one needs to be protected against. Where additional information is or can be made available to a contracting party, it may itself be subject to distortion. For example, surveyors' reports on houses, commissioned by house buyers, are often so heavily qualified – to protect the surveyor against subsequent legal action – that they lose much of their value.

The presence of asymmetric information in market transactions clearly raises a range of ethical issues relating to the ways in which market transactions are carried out which do not go away simply because mechanisms may exist to ameliorate their effects.

Another form of imbalance between buyer and seller may be in terms of the market power that they have. There are often occasions when there is a sole buyer or a sole seller. In these cases it is usually possible for the monopsonist or monopolist to exploit their uniqueness in a market transaction to their own advantage.

A third feature of a market is that it rarely exists in isolation from other markets. Indeed the economy may be seen as one vast contract map, consisting of a complex, interrelated set of markets. Activity in one market will almost certainly have implications for activity in others. This interrelatedness raises some important ethical issues. How far should I take knock-on effects in other markets into account when I contract as a buyer or seller in any particular market? When a buyer and seller are willing and able to conclude a legal contract in a particular market, is that the end of the matter? Or should either or both parties 'look behind' the contract between them? Does the conclusion of a legal contract limit my ethical responsibility for what is going on elsewhere in the production chain? It is not difficult to think of situations where these questions become important. For example, we may be aware that the new shoes we are proposing to buy might have involved child labour at some stage of production. The low price of the food I purchase may reflect near subsistence level wages for the primary producers. A farmer may know that the animals he sells at market may be badly treated in transport.

The simple point to be made here is that from a Christian perspective, there are no grounds for suggesting that moral responsibility is bounded by the legal scope of a contract.

SOME PRINCIPLES FOR MARKET PARTICIPATION

The previous section points to a need for us to think through, and then to apply, some of the basic principles which should guide our participation in markets. Five such principles are outlined below. These are not intended to constitute a comprehensive listing, but they are nevertheless likely to command widespread support among both Christians and non-Christians.

1. *We have a responsibility to look beyond the legal boundaries*

of a market contract.

Clearly it is not possible to delve into the detailed background of each market contract into which we enter. However, there will be times when we become aware of unsatisfactory elements in, for example, the supply chain, or we think further investigation is appropriate; these instances invite some response.

2. *We should act with integrity in market transactions.*

Deliberately misleading my contracting partner (e.g. by making false promises or claims, or by non-disclosure of key information); exploiting market power; or refusing to honour commitments, are obvious breaches of such a principle. There are of course times when it is unclear what 'acting with integrity' implies in practical terms; in these instances the arbiter must surely be a good conscience.

3. *We are primarily stewards, not owners of this world's resources.*

Christians seek to acknowledge God as the source of their well-being. We hold things in trust and we are called to use what we have for God's glory and for the good of others. The notion of stewardship has important implications for how we look at our possessions, our intellects and our skills. Stewardship responsibilities replace property rights.

Care for the God-created world is also a mark of good stewardship. Such care implies that the absence of well-defined property rights will not lead to the intentional generation of negative externalities.

Stewardship does of course take us back to the notions of interdependence and community again, since it is the good of others that is one of its primary goals.

4. *Service to others should be a characteristic of human activity.*

This principle lies at the heart of the Christian gospel, which proclaims a giving God, and a Saviour who gave himself for us. Christ's followers are called to wash one another's feet (Jn. 13:1–17). We are challenged to have a special concern for the hungry, the thirsty, the stranger, the naked, the sick and the imprisoned (Matt. 25:35–36). And at the workplace, we should provide respect for the dignity and well being of others.

5. *The essence of our lives does not consist in the things that we have.*

This principle is perhaps most clearly illustrated by the story of the foolish farmer in Luke 12. This farmer was overwhelmed by his own material success, and he decided that his response would be to take it easy and find his enjoyment in the things that he had acquired. Martin Luther King (King, 1963, p. 68) comments that this man's problem was not so much his wealth, but the fact that 'The economic structure of his life absorbed his destiny.' The farmer confused means with ends. Time and time again in the Gospels, Christ drives this message home. Christians are called to seek God's Kingdom first; everything else will be added afterwards. We can enjoy to the full all the good things that God has given us, but our treasure is elsewhere. It is perhaps interesting that allied with the farmer's preoccupation with his material state was his independence; he had no need for anyone else, an attitude destructive of any sense of community.

All of these principles have been under particularly strong attack over the last decade or so, and it is not easy to stand up for them in the prevailing economic climate. Nevertheless, we can seek to promote them politically and in all sorts of other ways. We may use them to evaluate market activities. But we may also use them to inform the way in which we ourselves participate in the market. For example, there is nothing to stop us from following John Wesley's exhortation (not without its own challenges!), given in a sermon on the Use of Money in 1744, to 'Gain all you can: save all you can: give all you can' (quoted in Harries, 1992, p. 76). Gains that are made in the market can be redistributed to others in more need.

We can also influence market outcomes by the way in which we participate in it as demanders and suppliers. There is no reason why part of what we 'demand' should not in turn reflect our perception of Christian values in relation to what is produced, how much is produced, and how it is produced. We may divert our demand away from goods and services which, for example, appear to exploit the powerless or vulnerable, or which are destructive of the environment, or which debase human nature.

We may also be willing to pay more for certain goods and services. For example, we may be prepared to pay a premium if we know that as a result poor producers will receive a higher wage. One way of interpreting such a premium is to see it as a payment for a particular product attribute that we favour. On the supply side, we may refuse to offer labour and other resources we own for certain types of productive behaviour. And if we are managers or owners, we can seek to conduct our business in a way that reflects Christian values.

SOME CONCLUDING REFLECTIONS

One of the implications of our discussion is that we should be careful about using the impersonal terms 'market' or 'market forces' as the source of values and motivations with which we are unhappy, and which we wish to change. Such usage can serve to deflect attention away from the ethical responsibilities of market *participants*. The fact that no one individual may be able to exercise a significant influence on market outcomes should not impede any challenge to the values and motivations that participants bring to the market place. It is against that background that we have looked at a number of basic principles for guiding behaviour in markets. How these principles are applied in practice is not at all easy, especially when there are trade-offs to be made, but working through these things represents a key (and exciting!) element in being a disciple in today's world.

Over the years, Traidcraft has sought to challenge, in a robust way, the values that are typically associated with market behaviour, and to demonstrate that alternative approaches are viable in a highly competitive and changing environment. A key element in Traidcraft's activities has been to bring into the international market place those producers who would not otherwise be there.

The history of the organisation shows that the fulfilment of Traidcraft's aims has not been easy or uncontroversial. Difficult and sometimes painful decisions have had to be made in balancing the needs of customers, producers, staff and the other groups associated with its work. Inevitably, too, there has been much debate over what 'fairness' in trade means in practice. Yet responding to these challenges should not be seen as somehow impeding Traidcraft's operation; it is in fact the stuff of its mission.

BIBLIOGRAPHY

Harries, R. (1992) *Is there a Gospel for the Rich?* Mowbray, London.
King, M.R (1963) *Strength to Love*, reprinted in Fount Paperbacks, 1977, London.
Block, W., Brennan, G. and Elzinga, K., eds. (1985) *Morality of the Market: Religious and Economic Perspectives*, Fraser Institute, Vancouver.
Sen, A (1999) *Development as Freedom*, Oxford University Press, Oxford.
Smith, A (1776) *An Inquiry into the Nature and Causes of the Wealth of Nations*, vols. I and II, edited by Edwin Cannan, 5th edn., 1950, first published as a University Paperback, 1961, Methuen, London.

NOTES

1   Revised version of a talk given to a joint meeting of the Boards of Traidcraft plc and Traidcraft Exchange and the Foundation Trustees, September 1999.
2   See Stuart Raistrick's piece later in this volume for a small sample of this literature.
3   Boulding (in Block et al., eds., 1985, p. 262) quotes the nursery rhyme: 'She liked coffee and I liked tea, and that was the reason we couldn't agree.' A market enables both parties to have what they want, without agreement between them.
4   This theme is also developed in Stuart Raistrick's chapter later in this book.
5   We should note that contrary to popular perception, Adam Smith's writings are not all about the wonders of the invisible hand. This phrase is only mentioned twice in the *Wealth of Nations*, and Smith was anxious to place market activities in a moral context.
6   Stuart Raistrick helpfully develops this theme further in Chapter Eight.

Chapter Three

Poverty-Reducing Development Strategies: Accepted and Neglected Challenges

Deryke Belshaw

INTRODUCTION

The purpose of this essay is to review the renewed openings and ongoing presures for pro-poor development activities on the part of both churches and Christian development agencies – faith-based organisations (FBOs) – in low income countries in 'the south'. The underlying themes are:

1. that in the poorer countries, the post-World War II experiment with state-led development and the introduction of universal semi-welfare states has become unsustainable;

2. that in responding to renewed opportunities for church-related inputs in the stressed social service sectors, especially education and health, the questions whether and how far the poor will benefit as a result have to be addressed at the outset and monitored over time; and

3. that the alternative strategy of assisting the poor to increase significantly their disposable incomes, thereby improving their access to the cost-sharing and user-fee mediated services, needs serious consideration at local decision-making levels.

The sequence of global events which have contributed to the stark choices facing a significant proportion of the world's poor people, and especially those in Sub-Saharan Africa (SSA), can be summarised into three distinctive but overlapping periods:

1. Between the end of World War II and the second oil price

shock in 1979 nearly all developing countries followed state-led development and welfare strategies with western or eastern block variants, that is more or less collectivism and central planning and greater or lesser emphasis on state-owned and protected industrialisation.

2. By the early 1980s the contribution of external economic shocks (energy prices, export commodity prices and interest rates) and problem-deepening internal policy responses (rigid, over-valued exchange rates, budget deficits and ensuing balance of payment crises, spiralling international debt and hyper-inflation) had made a series of radical economic policy reforms appear inevitable in the smaller and more open developing economies. Essentially the stabilisation and structural adjustment programmes rolled-back the development role of the state in favour of the private sector, with more emphasis after 1990 on anti-poverty measures in the form of employment 'safety nets', micro and small-scale projects implemented by non-government organisations (NGOs) and (rather paltry) compensation for retrenched state employees. Larger and less open economies, particularly India and China, and the Newly Industrialising Countries (NICs) of east and southeast Asia, where export oriented industrialisation strategies were proving successful, had less need of radical shifts in economic policy.

3. From the collapse of the eastern block in 1989, globalisation – the dominance of international market forces and institutions and reduced scope for independent national economic policies – is setting new ground rules for both developed and developing countries.

The accelerating pace of change is only partially captured in the following list of issues emerging over the last four or five years:

• The varied negative experiences of developing countries involved in (a) the 'Asian Crisis' from mid-1997, and (b) individual Latin American countries suffering from macro-economic and speculative financial crises – Mexico, Brazil and Peru in particular (see e.g. Stiglitz n.d.).

• The reduction of support by the World Bank for the so-called 'Washington Consensus' on strategy for economic adjustment, stabilisation and development (see for example,

Stiglitz 1998).
- The adoption by the Development Assistance Committee of the Organisation for Economic Co-operation and Development (the aid donors) of a set of poverty reducing targets for developing countries expressed not only in absolute income poverty terms, but also in a range of specific health, literacy and gender-based indicators, to be achieved by the year 2015.
- The accelerating decline in donor aid in favour of private investment (especially reduction in government-to-government aid) with partial replacement by donor grants and contracts awarded to NGOs.
- Increasing problems in maintaining effective global food security and the case for partial substitution of food aid by in-country food production subsidies and/or 'aid for food', that is financial assistance to increase capacity for commercial importation of staple foodstuffs in disaster situations.
- In the first international conference of the World Trade Organisation, which was held in Seattle, USA, towards the end of 1999, little progress was made in general, but in particular on the important issue for low-income countries of a phased dismantling of protective measures for temperate and Mediterranean zone agricultural products within the European Union.
- The generally poor track record of international peace-making and conflict resolution activities with organisational and funding issues reducing political commitment by the richer countries.
- Recent questions about whether micro-projects and micro-finance projects such as the Grameen Bank are likely to be either unsustainable or lead to displacement of pre-existing infrastructure or business when the local economy is stagnant.
- Doubts on the speed and effectiveness of the agreement reached by the creditor countries to expand the IMF's debt remission initiative from 20 to 40 poor countries and reduce the qualifying period from six years to three.

In the 1990s, the combined consequence of ineffective recovery programmes and globalisation trends on the economies of Sub-

Saharan Africa has been their marginalization. Stagnant or low growth economies accompanied by mass poverty have become the norm; trade and inward investment flows are well below historical levels in most countries. This situation, however, is not inevitable. Effective development strategies can be designed, funded and implemented if realistic analysis is carried out at the local and sub-national regional levels. To take two examples. Firstly, unlike the prevalent situation in Asian countries, in tropical Africa, fresh water – the key factor in the production of crops, animals and other products (including high protein sources of food such as fish, ducks and geese) – is not a managed resource. A wide range of low-cost appropriate technology for the 'harvesting' and application of water to enhance household production, consumption and real incomes remains unused. Secondly, in many schools and medical facilities staff attendance is so erratic that the quality of the teaching and health care provided is seriously impaired. This situation usually reflects the fact that the original 'full-time' salaries were eroded by hyper-inflation and have not been readjusted subsequently. Unless one of the available options to restore normal work discipline is introduced, the quality problem in social service delivery will remain.

The next two sections of this essay are intended to illustrate the realities of the African development malaise. The first provides data for the late 1990s indicating the prevalence of economic decline, income poverty and 'deschooling' in SSA. The next section illustrates the socially-embedded nature of new customs and attitudes which contribute to economic non-recovery situations; discussion relates to education, health services, physical infrastructure and the work ethic in the modern or formal sector. The following section summarises the evidence for favouring an initial strategic focus on achieving direct impact on income poverty through utilising under-used and under-regarded potential for increased output of agricultural tradable commodities by poor farm households and their individual members. The last substantive section examines the pattern of engagement in development activities generally adopted by churches and Christian development agencies in the light of the preceding discussion. Implications for the Church's holistic transformation policy and strategic choices are summarised in the concluding section.

THE ONGOING MARGINALISATION
OF SUB-SAHARAN AFRICAN ECONOMIES

In the great majority of SSA countries, mass absolute poverty – defined in relation to a poverty line or threshold of survival calculated in income per capita terms – is predominantly a rural phenomenon (see Table 1). It is caused by low or fluctuating levels of labour productivity in agrarian-based livelihoods. Concentrations of poor people are found especially in remote areas and regions prone to natural hazards. In a dozen or so countries, out of the fifty comprising SSA (World Bank, 1999a), the burden of ongoing wars or post-war recovery situations contribute significantly to the poverty problem.

Reader (1998) cites World Bank data that between 1965, when most African countries had achieved political independence, and 1980 when the second 'oil price shock' was affecting oil-importing economies, the average rate of economic growth per capita for SSA was 1.5 per cent per annum. This compared favourably with the equivalent figure for India which was 1.3 per cent. World Bank (1998) data, however, for the two periods 1980–90 and 1990–95 indicate the following pattern (for 34 SSA countries, omitting war-torn countries and 'small' countries with less than one million people):

- 1980–90: 19 countries (56 per cent) had negative GDP per capita growth rates, that is on average people were getting poorer;
- 1990–95: 23 countries (68 per cent) had negative GDP per capita growth. Of these, nine had had positive growth rates in the 1980-90 period. Only five countries which were negative in 1980-90 had returned to positive growth in 1990-95. In other words, an adverse situation at the SSA country level in the 1980s was deteriorating further in the first half of the 1990s.

Data covering the period 1990–98 (World Bank, 1999b) suggest that the total number of poor people (defined as living on less than US $1 per day) had risen from 242 million to 291

TABLE 1

INCOME POVERTY IN EIGHT AFRICAN COUNTRIES,
VARIOUS YEARS (1997–98)

Country and Period	Area	Percentage of population living below national poverty line*	
		First year	Last year
Burkina Faso 1994–98	Rural	51.1	50.7
	Urban	10.4	15.8
	Total	44.5	45.3
Ethiopia 1989–95 1994–97	Rural	61.3	45.9
	Urban	40.9	38.7
Ghana 1989–92	Rural	37.5	30.2
	Urban	19.0	20.6
	Total	31.9	27.4
Mauritania 1987–96	Rural	72.1	58.9
	Urban	43.5	19.0
	Total	59.5	41.3
Nigeria 1992–96	Rural	45.1	67.8
	Urban	29.6	57.5
	Total	42.8	65.6
Uganda 1992–97	Rural	59.4	48.2
	Urban	29.4	16.3
	Total	55.6	44.0
Zambia 1991–96	Rural	79.6	74.9
	Urban	31.0	34.0
	Total	57.0	60.0
Zimbabwe 1991–96	Rural	51.5	62.8
	Urban	6.2	14.9
	Total	37.5	47.2

* Based on national (nutritionally based) poverty lines. Comparisons between countries are not valid. *Source:* Demery (1999)

million; the proportion of poor people in the total population was virtually constant – 46.6 per cent in 1990, 46.3 per cent in 1998.

For eight SSA countries panel data allows the estimation of changes in rural, urban and total poverty over periods of three to nine years up to the late 1990s (Table 1). Four of these countries have registered a reduction in poverty, but two of these (Ethiopia and Uganda) reflect peace after long periods of destructive civil wars.

Alternative indicators of poverty prevalence measure access to basic services – primary education, health care and safe water supply. Table 2 reports eleven SSA countries where school enrolments have fallen below the 1980 baseline. The causes of these declines probably include several combinations of adverse factors:

- Falling parental real incomes.
- 'Cost-sharing' schemes, for example, parent-teacher association levies supplement eroded teachers salaries.
- Falling quality of classroom teaching.
- Declining employment and secondary/tertiary education opportunities.
- Rising relative labour productivity of children in intra-household employment.

A range of SSA country positions, in terms of poverty prevalence, is to be expected. Other studies indicate intra-country variation in poverty over time, between poor and non-poor groups (Sahn and Stifel, 1999), between urban and rural dwellers (Grootaert et al., 1998) and between different rural/agro-ecological areas (Belshaw et al., 1999). Strong upward recovery trends are noticeable by their absence.

THE DECLINE OF STATE WELFARISM IN AFRICA

In many SSA countries the decline in the provision of free basic social services is a fact of everyday life. Rarely has an announcement of an official change of policy been publicised in the media; the changes are gradual, incremental and insidious, affecting household real incomes, employment opportunities and social values in a variety of negative ways. The 'real world'

TABLE 2

SSA COUNTRIES REPORTING DECLINING EDUCATIONAL ENROLMENTS (%) 1980–93/5

Human Development Index † (1998)	Country *	Primary School Enrolment						All Levels Enrolment		
		Male			Female			Ages 6–23		
		1980	1993	Decline	1980	1993	Decline	1980	1995	Decline
153	Madagascar	139	75	46	133	72	46	60	33	45
169	Ethiopia	44	27	39	23	19	17	61	18	-13
150	Tanzania	99	71	28	86	69	20	44	34	23
137	Kenya	120	92	23	110	91	17	62	55	11
142	Nigeria	135	105	22	102	82	20	50	50	0
143	D R Kongo	#	#	—	#	#	—	46	38	17
144	Togo	146	122	16	91	81	11	61	50	18
148	Cote d'Ivoire	95	80	16	63	58	8	39	39	0
141	Comoros	#	#	—	#	#	—	45	39	13
133	Ghana	89	83	7	71	70	1	48	44	8
132	Cameroon	107	#	—	89	#	—	48	46	4

* Countries are ranked in descending order of severity of decline of male primary school enrolment or, if the data are not available, of all levels of enrolment.

\# Data not available.

† UNDP.

Sources: World Bank (1997: 226);UNDP (1998: 148)

in four important areas of socio-economic activity is discussed briefly in this section. These areas are: primary education, primary health care, local physical infrastructure and work patterns in the formal sector, namely government, large-scale business and large non-governmental institutions. Incidentally, a similar theme could be applied to some Asian countries. The generally acknowledged failure of the welfare state in India – the so called 'Nehrovian project' – is examined in a recently published collection of studies entitled *Illfare in India* (Harriss-White, 1999).

With respect to the provision of primary school education in the poorer SSA countries, for example the countries listed in Table 2, the official policy of free provision of school places is maintained as fees continue not to be charged. But parents have had to supplement the diminishing real resources in the education budget by paying a subscription to the parent-teachers' association (which may contribute the major share of teachers' salaries), paying for textbooks and exercise books, buying their children's school uniforms and providing midday meals. Even so, there is a risk that teachers are absent from school on other employment from which to supplement their perceived low remuneration as teachers. The rising real cost to parents of education is particularly likely to lead to under-enrolment of children of poorer parents and of girl pupils. At the same time, a system of bursaries and exemptions is either not in place (it is not required as education is 'free') or it often operates in an arbitrary manner with respect to objective merit and need criteria. Generally, poorer parents are concentrated in the rural sector, especially in remoter and less highly developed areas. A widening gap is being created between these areas, with high illiteracy, high fertility rates and less ability to diversify their livelihood dependence on the natural resource base (which may be coming under stress from population pressure) and the relatively richer rural and urban areas. The formation of an elite class is being accelerated and deepened on the basis of differential access to education and to the higher income opportunities for which educational achievement is the key.

Access to 'free' modern medical services is similarly fenced off by fee charges for treatment by doctors and nurses and the need to purchase medicines, which were previously supplied without payment. These charges are sometimes part of an official policy change to a 'cost-sharing' system. But at the same time, low-cost consultations or drugs may simply be unavailable at the public hospitals and dispensaries, the patient being referred to private consulting rooms, clinics and pharmacies run on a 'for profit' basis. The main consequences are again felt by the poorer people who are often forced to rely on traditional medical knowledge. This may provide effective cures for specific ailments, for example, various plant or herbal remedies, but the scientific understanding of causality is replaced by spirit-world explanations often reinforcing the hold on uneducated minds of repressive and superstitious cosmologies. The challenge to the church's ministries of physical, mental and spiritual healing, therefore, comes from reinvigorated traditional belief systems consequent on the withdrawal of access from the poorer groups of state-mediated scientific medical services.

The third area of distress arising from welfare service decline is the inability of either the state or local communities to bear the maintenance costs of previously provided physical infrastructure. Roads, bridges, domestic water supply plant, schools and dispensaries, especially in rural areas, and sewage disposal, electricity systems and telephone networks have been poorly maintained and have become unreliable or inoperable in many African countries. This form of development was not established on a sustainable basis.

Comprehensive data on the size of this problem is not available, but the 1998 UNDP data source indicated five countries reporting a decline in the proportion of population served by safe water sources (see Table 3). In the cases of Congo, Tanzania and Burkina Faso, the lower proportion of population served may largely reflect failure to continue expanding public water supply coverage at or above the rate of population growth. But in the case of Zambia and Malawi a significant breakdown in installed scheme-delivery seems to have occurred. Two general points are that (a) user charges need to be levied from service beneficiaries at the level required to maintain the function provided over the long term, with the institutional arrangements and trained manpower capacity put in place; and (b) the ability of communities to maintain the existing physical infrastructure and, hopefully, further additions to it over time, depends on raising their productivity and disposable cash incomes. This may require a multi-sector or strategic framework designed at the community, area or local government level. As this should reflect people's needs and priorities, setting up a number of participatory assemblies would be desirable.

TABLE 3

SSA COUNTRIES REPORTING
DECLINING ACCESS TO SAFE WATER (%)

UNDP Human development index	Country *	1975–80	1990–96
146	Zambia	42	27
161	Malawi	51	37
172	Burkina Faso	25	22
128	Congo	38	34
150	Tanzania	39	38

* Countries are ranked in descending order of severity of decline. *Source:* UNDP *(1998: 148)*

Finally, the high rates of inflation during the early part of the economic crisis of the 1980s usually led to a rapid fall in real wages in the public sector and in the formal part of the private sector. Most public sector rates of remuneration have only partly recovered to the present time. A common reaction in the professional and middle management cadres was to find one or more additional part-time contracts or occupations. Taxi-driving university lecturers exist and more frequently one encounters the 'second jacket syndrome' in a government or university office. The jacket is draped on the chair behind the office desk and if a secretary is available to explain where the incumbent is, one is told 'well, as you can see, he has just popped out'. 'Popping out' may extend up to several days if work is pressing in other businesses. The effect is to probably cut value productivity (but real wages have fallen as well as output) and particularly to reduce institutional capacity. Since the moral consensus about this practice is usually summed up by the phrase 'one's children must eat', no moral censure can be applied, work discipline is largely absent and the self-reliance principle can be extended without compunction to supplementing wages from institutional resources (stocks of spare parts are sold off; library books are sold for wrapping paper, etc.). One obvious solution would be for the employer to substitute, apologetically, a part-time contract equivalent to the pre-crisis rate per day while registering no objection to other part-time work being done outside the times of work specified in the new contract. The value of free or subsidised housing occupied by the employee can also be factored in to the new contract. Employers I have discussed this problem with (including the managers of a church-run hospital) have agreed with the solution in principle but say that they could not act without government backing, whether by edict or legislation. In effect, therefore, the restoration of a normally-functioning moral economy may be blocked by the self-interest or inertia of some politicians and / or civil servants occupying key positions.

THE PRO-POOR ALTERNATIVE STRATEGY: AGRICULTURAL TRADABLES-LED DEVELOPMENT

The effectiveness of small-scale agricultural development in achieving significant impact on poverty has been widely demonstrated (Bourguinon and Morrisson, 1998). Even in the face of external shocks and often long periods with an overvalued domestic currency (which reduces the incentive for tradables production), a small number of African countries have been able to achieve dramatic commodity export growth. This has enabled them to share to advantage in expanding world trade, using it to regain or sustain economic growth and to generate incomes for small producer households and wage earners. Table 4 shows the leading country/crop cases of significant and

TABLE 4

PHYSICAL OUTPUT OF SELECTED AGRICULTURAL TRADABLES
1971–73 (A) TO 1996–98 (B) [THOUSAND TONNES]

	Cotton		Cocoa		Tobacco		Tea		Sugar	
	A	B	A	B	A	B	A	B	A	B
Benin	18	172								
Cameroon									236	1350
Cote d'Ivoire			207	1165						
Kenya							49	253	1642	4600
Malawi					29	153			377	1787
Mali	23	188								

Source: Lawrence and Belshaw (1999)

sustained expansion of tradable goods production found in a study of 14 African countries (Lawrence and Belshaw, 1999).[1] There were 33 country/commodity cases in the study. The best eight cases show overall output increases in the range from 280 to 970 per cent over the 25-year period 1971–73 to 1996–98. The resulting income terms of trade gains seem likely to offset any adverse price trend (which is a long-term phenomenon in any case). The 'fallacy of composition' argument[2] has to be assessed against potential world market growth; clearly in the short term, countries influenced by the fallacy argument have lost out to those countries which ignored it. In half of these cases output was steadily advancing over the whole period. Of the others, the three sugar cases recorded major growth 'spurts' over shorter periods, mainly in the 1970s; this doubtless reflects the 'lumpy' nature of investment in integrated sugar mill capacity and the associated irrigated cane estates, the dominance of transnational corporation (TNC) activity in the sub-sector and the deterioration in the investment climate in sub-Saharan Africa from the early 1980s. In the case of cotton expansion in Benin, much the greater part, surprisingly, occurred in the twelve-year period 1979–81 to 1991–93, when currency over-valuation was severe throughout the 13 country CFA Franc zone.

Both area expansion and improved technology, especially high-yielding planting material, have been instrumental in raising production. The former involves, of course, a cost from the loss of output from the previous land use, but this is certainly less, and is often minimal, compared with the lead enterprise. The most striking institutional feature in all eight cases is their association with single-commodity vertically integrated production, processing and marketing systems. This may involve production being located on large estates, but more usually on small- and medium-sized family farms or on a combination of the two. The linkage of low-cost small-holder producers to economies of large-scale processing and marketing through 'outgrower' or 'nucleus estate' arrangements has been successfully demonstrated for tea and sugar production in many eastern and southern African countries by the Commonwealth Development Corporation, a bilateral parastatal investment corporation (CDC, various years). In these cases, smallholders are grouped into self-managing cooperative societies but alternative systems using agri-business contracts or primary buyers financed by TNC exporters may be more appropriate or equally efficient in other contexts. The general term small-to-large enterprises (SLEs) is proposed to designate this class of institutional network. It is also noteworthy that no successful cases emerged from the historically prevalent horizontally-coordinated structures of public sector extension, research, cooperative and statutory marketing board networks.[3]

It is clear, however, that in trying to accelerate the tradable commodity engine of growth, neither national nor international private agencies are likely to succeed on their own, that is without location-specific cooperation with the public sector. This is especially the case where there is a need to provide bottleneck-breaking infrastructure in rural areas, for example, under decentralised area-based programmes. Roads and bridges, irrigation works and selective electrification, as well as ensuring physical security, are usually public sector responsibilities. Their planned provision is a precondition for increased private sector activity to materialise. Public-private partnership (PPP) arrangements of various kinds require greater attention generally, but especially for poverty-reducing agricultural and rural development, land reform, tourism and social safety net activities. NGOs (including FBOs) may also have an important role to play here (see Alsop et al. 1999 for an Indian case study). The relevant, but neglected, interface between the local and the national levels of development strategy is the sub-national region (Belshaw, 2000). The issue of appropriate network processes and structures at the regional level requires recognition and resources if the potential of participatory procedures at the local level is to be realised.

It is necessary to acknowledge that the assembly of experiences in this field from which to improve performance through networking and training has hardly yet begun. The array of significant gaps which require formal research *ex post,* as well as ongoing pilot studies or action research, is forbiddingly large. Questions of access to information and joint funding of research by or for interested stakeholders has to be negotiated.

In this chapter it is only possible to nominate some of the more pressing research areas in rather staccato fashion. They include:

- What are the experiences and lessons with different types of SLE arrangements? What reforms can be introduced into existing institutions to ensure greater impact on the poverty reduction objective?

- In similar vein, what lessons can be learned from (the few) PPP arrangements at national, regional and, possibly, local level? Can pro-poor improvements be effected in some of them even at an early stage in their implementation?

- What are the possibly constructive relationships that can be introduced between civil society organisations (CSOs), especially community-based organisations (CBOs) and faith-based organisations (FBOs) on the one hand and private sector agencies on the other? For example, the effective and fair operation of PPPs can be seriously damaged in a pervasive climate of low-level corruption. Could FBOs play a constructive role as part of a wider network of development agencies (see CAPA/World Bank 2000 and Belshaw et al. (eds.) 2001 for illustrations of this type of approach)?

- What are the implications for agri-business growth in SSA of the increasing importance of ethical consumerism in world markets? Questions about producer remuneration, labour standards, food quality, environmental issues etc.. may be easier to satisfy in well-supported smallholder agriculture than in large-scale commercial operations. Can/will private exporters use these new opportunities to the advantage of African poor people?

- What role may there be for ethical investment in agri-business – especially in local-level path-breaking ventures?[4] Slow-return enterprises, such as fruit and nut tree crops which generate complementary environmental benefits through the effects of agro-forestry systems on soil and water conservation functions, may prove particularly suitable.

- What are the possible macro-economic effects of rising disposable incomes in poor households, especially for taxable capacity at central and decentralised government level? What balance between private and public expenditure on

social services would raise the quality of provision in them?
• How might published research articles and strategic demonstration effects from successful SLE and PPP arrangements reduce the intellectual climate of opposition in African and international development circles to agricultural and peasant economy-based solutions to economic recovery and poverty problems?

CHRISTIAN CONTRIBUTIONS TO POVERTY REDUCTION

THROUGH A GLASS DARKLY

We are now in a position to begin to examine the question 'how far is the church playing an adequate pro-poor strategic role'. For two reasons this, again, is restricted to SSA. Firstly, income poverty is already widespread there and is growing most rapidly of all the macro-regions of the world. Secondly, at present this question can only be approached on the basis of personal experience, since a statistically reliable survey of both coverage and quality of Christian development impacts is not available – this deserves the highest priority for research attention in the context of growing opportunities and responsibilities available for the church to renew its historical pro-poor holistic mission (see CAPA/World Bank 2000 and Belshaw et al. (eds) 2001). The experiential frame of reference which I can bring to the task is necessarily limited: work in only 17 SSA countries, mainly anglophone; Christian NGOs (Association of Evangelicals in Africa, Stromme Foundation, Traidcraft, World Vision, amongst others). The time framework extends from periodic contacts with three mission societies in the field when a resident in Northern Nigeria in 1955–56 to work for the Council of Anglican Provinces in Africa in Nigeria and Kenya in 1999–2000; within that period co-convening the first interdenominational conference (funded by the United Nations Children's Fund – UNICEF) on Christian rural development projects in East Africa (Watts, 1969). So, at best, one might expect a basis for discussion and constructive disagreement, leading to a more representative knowledge and deeper understanding of the diversity of the African church's experience with development activities and strategies. We concentrate on the experience from 1980 onwards when, as already described, the poorly appraised development and welfare state strategies which the world powers wished upon the governments of Africa began to unravel.

Whilst focusing explicitly on socio-economic, environmental and political dimensions of holistic transformation, there is a danger of overlooking the liberating and empowering impacts of the spiritual gospel in many areas of the everyday life of poor people. This requires, amongst other things, that the good news is conveyed intelligibly to them and they are not excluded from compassionate, caring Christian community life.

PARTIALLY ACCEPTED CHALLENGES

Those challenges to reduce poverty that the church in Africa has most widely accepted fall, it is suggested, into two categories. The first consists of service delivery in the social sectors, especially health and education. The second category entails the advocacy of reforms expected to lead to economic justice for groups of poor people within countries or for poor nations in the international context; the main reform issues are gender equality, high-level corruption, conflict resolution, international debt relief and fair trade.

Curative health services run by church agencies in general have good reputations for the quality of care and often reduce or waive charges for poorer patients. Nevertheless, the capacity of the church to replace public health services, rather than fill an expanding but still supporting role, must be in doubt. Nor may it be the highest health priority. As we have seen, poor people faced with cost-sharing or privatisation of modern health services are forced to rely on traditional medical practices. Whilst some natural chemotherapeutic measures are efficacious, the associated belief systems are antithetical to the analyses of medical science and, normally, to Christian religion also. Can the church provide decentralised primary health care – both preventative and curative – which costs less and is more effective than either traditional medicine or modern private or public health services?

In the face of the HIV/AIDS pandemic, the most effective prevention is secured by Christian sexual mores embracing lifetime chastity and fidelity (Okaalet 2000). The provision of expert knowledge confronting both traditional or transitional customs and beliefs and ex-western commercialised youth culture is urgently required. In the light of positive impact on sexual mores achieved by this approach, what manpower and funding are required to achieve effective protection for the vast numbers of young, poor Africans who are most at risk of becoming new HIV victims? Perhaps it would be fair to say that the church is accepting the health challenge, but on too small a scale and at too high levels of unit cost to achieve the needed impacts.

Modern educational services at all levels were supplied by the church in Africa often before the public sector, and a residual role and influence has often been retained. In poorer countries, cases of governments handing back responsibilities – or even asking that new facilities be opened – are quite frequent. The financial charges levied on parents to achieve competitive quality of teaching, that is for progression by pupils to the end of tertiary education (and possibly employment), are beyond the reach of poor families' current incomes unless bursaries are available. But in any case, the ability of African economies to provide employment for graduates, let alone secondary school drop-outs, varies with the size and growth rate of the formal or modern sector, mortality rates for the educated employed adults and the size of the net annual brain drain relative to the output from the educational institutions. In poorer countries, therefore, it would be realistic to acknowledge two related problems: the low probability of modern sector employment facing tertiary and secondary level leavers, and the disaffection that academic syllabi impart to unemployed leavers faced only with low wage or self employment in the rural sector and the urban informal sector. The real educational challenge, therefore, is to substitute low cost literacy and vocational training for academic courses in classrooms. This new training should as far as possible be 'on-the-job' and combine local indigenous technical knowledge, appropriate technology and applied scientific knowledge (Green, 2000). Demonstration projects where the missing cadres of trainers of teacher trainers and teacher trainers and teachers can be instructed are needed to accelerate the otherwise lengthy process of educational syllabus reform. The challenge facing Christians who venerate academic education – whether for the material benefits it has brought them or for its intrinsic merits – is to critique its inappropriate dominance in those economies which can neither bear its cost nor use its output productively and which becomes a key device for excluding the poor from formal sector jobs.

Advocacy against gender inequality is increasingly made by groups – mainly women's groups – within the African church. Whether uniform laws can provide economic justice for wealthy families with, for example, two modern sector incomes, on the one hand, and poor families with barely adequate or insufficient asset bases for survival and with necessarily extensive joint consumption within the family on the other, seems questionable. Other arenas for advocacy – corruption in high places, conflict resolution and debt relief – require coalitions between northern and southern churches, NGOs and pressure groups with religious or secular belief systems. The issue of good governance is being linked by the donors to debt relief; for how long the poor should suffer the ongoing burden of international debt[5] because of the incompetence or venality of their political classes has not been widely addressed. It seems to be a suitable topic for the worldwide church to examine further. Christian NGOs, of course, have spearheaded the Jubilee 2000 alliance on debt relief, and useful work on this subject has been published recently both in the UK and the USA by Christian economists (Menzies 2000; Smith et al. 2000). Neither making satisfactory progress on debt relief itself, nor renewing development at acceptable rates of progress, are likely to be short-run processes; there will be opportunities to learn from experience and thereby to increase the effectiveness of impact sequentially.

MAINLY NEGLECTED CHALLENGES

It is suggested that the major areas of opportunity for, but in general neglect by, the church are as follows:
- Enhancing the real incomes and sustainable livelihoods of

the poor: the World Bank itself has drawn attention to the gross underfunding of development in Africa's rural regions (World Bank, 1996: 10–13). This situation would lend itself to informed advocacy activities undertaken by the local and international churches and Christian NGOs. Also, recent reviews of development research findings take an 'export optimism' view of the prospects for expanding labour-intensive commodity production, especially in Africa (Humphrey and Morrisson, 2000; Wood, 2000). The implementation of innovatory pilot projects demonstrating the ability of commodity export growth to raise the incomes of the poor directly, as described earlier in this chapter, should be within the competency of the church, acting usually as part of a network of relevant local development agencies.

- Networking with other development agencies at local and sub-national regional levels: in particular, the church could activate links with Christian businesses and sources of development finance, as well as with public sector agencies and Christian NGOs. In one African diocese, a UN-funded project, implemented by the church, enabled needed advice and planting material to reach poor farmers by paying for the costs of government transport; the agricultural official's time was gladly supplied at no extra charge! Such collaboration is not commonly encountered.

- Gender inequality: at the heart of the problem of gender inequality lies the question, what is best for all members of the family, for present and future generations? What kind of changes, lightening women's burdens and raising their dignity, would most improve the quality of family life for all its members? The church is uniquely equipped to find the range of answers to these practical questions relating to identified contexts.

- The problems of distorted moral economy and 'low-level' corruption: the examples of these problems described previously require discussion and action in the church's own institutions, which would then provide examples for adoption in wider society. Unrealistic perceptions of socio-economic norms, often based on exaggerated notions of the power of governments, need to be replaced through teaching and discussion based on accurate socio-economic information.

- Conflict prevention: conflict resolution is ameliorative, coming after a lot of damage has been done. Prevention, whether at local or international level, requires more attention by the church for obvious reasons. In large parts of Africa, continuing population growth will intensify competition over natural resources – land, water, vegetation, fish stocks, etc. Early identification of prevention possibilities – establishing quota shares and/or increasing resource productivity, monitoring infringements and bringing offenders before the legal authorities – are aspects the church could both advocate and participate in especially on behalf of the poor and weaker groups in society.

- Church sustainability: churches themselves have to work out their own sustainability strategy, with money and professionalism the key resource issues. Can New Testament stewardship and resource management principles be applied in their original or modified forms to particular contexts? How large and expensive do the overhead structures of churches need to be? Would greater variation in roles and structures of the churches provide for better sustainability and more appropriate interaction with the poor in the local community?

- Other neglected areas with strong implications for the role and content of Christian pro-poor activities include:
  - All aspects of unfair and even life-threatening international trade arrangements affecting low-income countries, such as aspects of the European Union's common agricultural policy (CAP) and the cartelisation of crude oil prices (up by 300 per cent in the first six months of 2000).
  - The strategic balance between welfarist or 'compassionate' approaches to poverty reduction (Ette, 2000) on the one hand and directly income generating activities for poor people (and therefore tax revenue and foreign exchange earning or saving at the same time) on the other. Aspects of poverty reduction that have received partial or no attention to date can be picked up in macro-regional, national and local forums in Africa. The evaluation of ongoing and new interventions and policy reforms will provide, even more powerfully, opportunities for 'learning by doing' and

the selection by the church and its co-operating partners of increasingly effective poverty-reducing strategies.

CONCLUSION

It is clear that, even restricting ourselves to SSA, there can be no one single conclusion, recommending one specific strategy, which will reduce absolute poverty across the continent. We have referred to an economic continuum of countries; some which are less poor, such as Gabon or Botswana, may be able to resuscitate and sustain the semi-welfare state. But for the majority, difficult ethical and development decisions must be made about what is possible and what is needed. A degree of shift of strategy to raise directly poor people's productivity and incomes seems necessary. The church needs to establish the research and analytical capacities to identify the ethically-superior options for resource allocation and socio-economic transition trajectories which will include the poor as the major beneficiaries.

Addressing these components of transformational development which are concerned with the reduction of human material, cultural and spiritual poverty requires both positive or diagnostic analyses and, of course, normative or prognostic prescriptions of probable problem solutions at various levels from the global to the local. The disciplinary perspectives and skills required cannot be restricted to those of economics alone, even in its broadest sense. The moral and ethical grounds of economic justice have to be identified and agreed (see Mott and Sider, 2000). The results of technical and micro-economic studies in the key sectors, such as agriculture, business, energy and transport, as well as medicine and hygiene, education and water supply, amongst others, are likely to make significant contributions. Studies in applied theology which integrate spiritual dimensions with the material and cultural factors in multi-disciplinary analyses, are extremely rare at present, underlining the urgent need for further data collection and team research work.

At the final decision-making stage, when alternative pro-poor strategies, projects and practices need to be appraised, the call for economics inputs is likely to re-emerge. This is because in materially poor countries, the use of appraisal criteria such as financial efficiency and cost-effectiveness are helpful in avoiding, for example, the selection of 'best-practice' solutions which can be afforded only by a minority or which cannot be financially, environmentally and/or institutionally self-sustaining. Nevertheless, in the context of economic development, with its mixed equity (including poverty reduction), growth (efficiency) and environmental objectives, economics must play a collaborative and synthesising rather than a dominant role. But then a servanthood function should not be a strange practice for Christian economists, at least!

BIBLIOGRAPHY

Alsop, R., Gilbert, E., Farrington, J. and Khandelwal, R. (2000) *Coalitions of Interest: partnerships for processes of agricultural change*. New Delhi: Sage.

Belshaw, D. (2000) 'Decentralised Governance and Poverty Reduction: relevant experience in Africa and Asia', in Collins, P. (ed.), *Applying Public Administration in Development.* Chichester: Wiley, pp. 93–113.

Belshaw, D., Calderisi, R. and Sugden, C. (eds.) (2001) *Faith in Development: Church-World Bank Collaboration in Poverty Reduction in Sub-Saharan Africa*. Washington, D.C.: World Bank and Oxford: Regnum International (in press).

Belshaw, D., Lawrence, P. and Hubbard, M. (1999) 'Agricultural Tradables and Economic Recovery in Uganda: the limitations of structural adjustment in practice', *World Development, 27.* 4, pp. 673–690.

Bourguinon, F. and Morrison, C. (1998) 'Inequality and Development: the role of dualism', *Journal of Development Economics, 57.* pp. 233–257.

CAPA / World Bank (2000) The Churches and Poverty Reduction in Africa: Communiqué of the Nairobi Conference. *Transformation 17.* 4.

C.D.C. (var. years), *Annual Report*. London: Commonwealth Development Corporation.

Demery, L. (1999) *Poverty Dynamics in Africa: an update* (draft). Washington, D.C.: World Bank.

Ette, Mercy(2000) 'Usurers Seek Blessings', *NewsAfrica,* 5–18 June.

Green, David (2000) 'Small Farm Households at the Cutting Edge: appropriate technology and sustainable rural development', *Transformation, 17.* 2, pp. 70–74.

Grootaert, C. et al. (1997) 'The Dynamics of Welfare Gains and Losses: an African case study', *Journal of Development Studies, 33.* 5, pp. 635–637.

Harriss-White, Barbara (ed.) (1999) *Illfare in India.* New Delhi: Sage.

Humphrey, J. and Morrissey, O. (2000) 'Add Value, Go Global: Can southern firms break into export markets?', *Development Research Highlights, 33.*

International Monetary Fund (1999) 'Structural Adjustment in Sub-Saharan Africa is Focus of High-level Regional Gathering: Bank of Mauritius – IMF Institute Seminar', *IMF Survey, 28.* 13, pp. 216–7.

Lawrence, P. and Belshaw, D. (1999) 'The Non-recovery of Agricultural Tradables and Enduring Rural Poverty in Sub-Saharan Africa.' 4th Inter-University Colloquium of the Standing Committee on University Studies of Africa, University of East Anglia, Norwich.

Menzies, G. (2000) 'The Economics and Ethics of International Debt Relief', *Journal of the Association of Christian Economists,* 27, pp. 1–16.

Mott, S. and Sider, R.J. (2000) 'Economic Justice: a Biblical paradigm', *Transformation, 17.* 2, pp. 50–63.

Okaalet, P. (2000) 'Reducing Poverty through Combating HIV/AIDS', *Transformation, 17.* 4.

Reader. J. (1998) *Africa: a biography of the continent.* Harmondsworth: Penguin.

Sahn, D.E. and Stifel. D.C. (1999) 'Poverty Comparisons over Time and across Countries in Africa. Ithaca', Cornell University.

Smith, S.L.S. *et al.* (2000) 'Christian Ethics and the Forgiveness of Third World Debt: a symposium', *Faith and Economics,* 35. pp. 8–19.

Stiglitz, J. (1998) 'More instruments and broader goals: moving towards the post – Washington concensus', *World Institute of Development Economics Research Lectures No. 2.* Helsinki: United Nations University.

Stiglitz, J. (n.d.) 'What I learned at the World Economic Crisis. The Insider.' Mimeo.

United Nations Development Programme (1998) *Human Development Report, 1998.* New York: Oxford University Press.

Watts, E.R. (1969) *New Hope for Rural Africa.* Nairobi: East African Publishing House.

Wood, A. (2000) 'Land versus Labour: Diverging paths of export growth', *Development Research Highlights*, 33.

World Bank (1996) *Taking Action to Reduce Poverty in Sub-Saharan Africa: an overview.* Washington D.C.

World Bank (1997) *World Development Report, 1997: The state in a changing world.* New York: Oxford University Press.

World Bank (1998) *World Development, 1998*: New York: Oxford University Press.

World Bank (1999a) *World Development Report, 1999/2000: entering the 21st century.* New York: Oxford University Press.

World Bank (1999b) *Poverty Trends and the Voices of the Poor.* Washington D.C.

World Bank (2000, forthcoming) *World Development Report, 2000/2001: Attacking Poverty.* New York: Oxford University Press.

NOTES

1   The number of country-commodity cases was constrained by the availability of data sets extending from the pre-OPEC shocks baseline through to the late 1990s. Current work, involving alternative data sources and relaxation of the strict time comparability condition, will allow considerably more country-commodity cases to be examined.

2   The argument that it is not profitable for one country to expand its production of an export commodity because other producing countries will do likewise; the combined increase in supply will depress the international price of the commodity assuming static and inelastic demand and thus reduce total revenue received. This ignores any gains from reduction in the cost of production.

3   The viability of the latter system is affected by the macro-context and especially the presence of parallel economies and pervasive low-level corruption in public life. The author's experience as a member of the two international economic recovery missions to Uganda – in 1979 and 1986 – can serve to illustrate the point: after four years of economic collapse, it seemed possible in 1979 to restore the public horizontal system to working efficiency; after eleven years of mayhem – in 1986 – it did not; the alternative vertical system was recommended and put in place between 1991 and 1998.

4   The introduction of cotton into Uganda in the early 1900s, the

major export commodity until overtaken by coffee in the 1960s, is attributed to an Anglican Christian investment company (The Uganda Company, Limited). Similar combinations of faith, trade and welfare objectives are found elsewhere in Africa, e.g. Lutheran Churches and smallholder coffee production in what has become Tanzania.

5   While some of this debt can be attributed to national policy or implementation errors, significant causality can be objectively attributed also to OPEC and to the policy responses of industrialised countries in the face of higher energy prices in the period 1980 to 1983 especially.

Part II

Traidcraft's Experience and Future

Chapter Four

Beginnings and Intentions

Richard Adams

Traidcraft, quite naturally, grew out of a greengrocer's shop. Initially, Turner's Stores in north-west London was the base for a small business importing vegetables from small farmers in developing countries. Conceived in outline five years earlier and run by three college friends, it was almost certainly the only greengrocer's shop run by a clergyman, an agricultural economist and a sociologist. Begun in the year when OPEC flexed its muscle, the oil crisis of 1974, with its rise in air freight costs, meant a shift towards higher value products with a greater labour content. A fortuitous meeting with a Baptist missionary from Bangladesh hastened this process, and jute macrame from the Ganges delta began to flood Britain via north London. It remains a tribute to the evangelical relief agency, TEAR Fund, that it effectively bank-rolled Traidcraft's predecessor, Tearcraft, as it made the transition from courgettes to crafts. Five years of tension, in management and theology, eventually led to a break and Traidcraft's birth in 1979. The challenges, achievements and difficulties of that five year period leading to the formation of Traidcraft, have continued to be reflected up to the present day.

It was impossible that Traidcraft should not reflect various views of Christian mission, social and political concern. One aspect was a largely traditional approach. In the 1970s the relief agency, TEAR Fund, represented, for development-orientated evangelical Christians, the expression of the command to go into the world and preach the gospel. As a development agency, its concern was with the physical well-being of people, but it reassured its largely theologically conservative supporters that this did not mean neglecting the spiritual, as its aid and development programmes were in the hands of Christian partners in the developing world.

Another perspective came from its progenitors. Michael Schluter, the agricultural economist, has subsequently founded the Jubilee Centre, the Keep Sunday Special Campaign and the Relationships Foundation. Tim McClure, the clergyman, is now Archdeacon of Bristol. In some respects a deep analysis of Traidcraft's Christian roots and ethos can be short-circuited. Its founders were young, radical Christians seeking to apply their faith in their work.

Seeking to bring faith and ethics into business is not new. For well over two hundred years, radicals and Christians, occasionally combining both dimensions, have applied their principles to trade and business. The industrial revolution brought dramatic changes and those with a social conscience felt compelled to respond. Sometimes this resulted in attempts to reform factory and working conditions, sometimes in the creation of new model businesses, like those founded by the Quaker chocolateers, and infrequently in early consumer boycotts of unethically sourced products, though it took the slave trade to stir early nineteenth-century British scruples about sugar plantations.

Back in the days when industrial capitalism was flexing its muscles, fair trade and free trade were seen as two sides of the same coin. Free trade became significant as a means to cheap food and sale of manufactures. Consumer power, first evident in the Corn Law protests, rapidly came of age through direct engagement with manufacturing, land ownership and retailing. Fair trade found its expression initially in the Rochdale Pioneers of 1844, not the first co-operative retailing venture but the first to succeed, growing rapidly into the hugely successful Co-operative Retail and Wholesale Movements of the late nineteenth century. Alongside the 'Store', unionism was also gaining strength as a response to the power and abuses of the new system.

CO-OPERATIVES AND CONSUMERS

When the first co-op store opened the world was populated by one billion people. The early co-operators were particularly concerned to provide unadulterated food and fair weights and measures but there was also a strong dose of political awareness. As the basic concerns of the British consumer were met and people began to get healthier and live longer, the first stirrings of contemporary consumer action arose in America. By the 1930s, the world population had doubled to two billion and this coincided with the founding of the US Consumers' Union – looking at quality, reliability and value for money, the 'higher' though only tangentially ethical consumer values.

By the time the Consumers' Association was established in Britain in the late 1950s, world population was up to three billion and this was the point at which we can identify the first specific alternative trade organisation, SOS Wereldhandel in Holland. The fifteen years from 1975 was perhaps the most dynamic and formative period for the fair trade movement. The lead-up was a decade of rising affluence and global awareness, decolonisation and the founding of UNCTAD (United Nations Commission on Trade and Development) in 1964. The founding of Traidcraft and its European counterparts came at a time when global population had reached four billion and rising with no limit in sight: when materialism was delivering wide-scale material prosperity in the first world and when it was also clear that the gap between rich and poor was growing wider; and when the power of the global corporation had never been greater; but when that power was benefitting the wealthy rather than those on the margins.

So here, as best as I can disentangle them, are reflections on the strands that shaped Traidcraft in the years immediately before and after its foundation.

PERSONAL REFLECTIONS

One of those strands is personal. I left college in 1968, the year of European student protest, possibly the only graduate to have simultaneously taken a degree in sociology and a diploma in theology from different universities 275 miles apart. And I wanted to change the world. I had just decided that training for the priesthood in the Church of England was a mistake. I was not going through a crisis of faith or a sudden awakening of social conscience, just a realisation that there was an alternative way of combining belief and action. It seemed to me that being radical was not primarily about Latin radishes or being at one pole or the other but about being *different*. Living in a college where many of the students were planning to enter Christian ministry, I had found myself positioned, though thankfully not pinioned, between the bibliolatory of the evangelical and the ecclesiolatory of the catholic.

Christians inevitably read into the person of Jesus things prompted by their own life experience and psychological development. We also extend this process into our perception of church structures, or those of Christian organisations. One of the features of Traidcraft which I certainly welcomed and encouraged was that it did have a largely cross-tradition appeal; indeed an appeal that extended well beyond faith communities of whatever background into non-religious humanism. Faith is an area where objectivity is not only impossible to achieve but counter-intuitive to practice. For me, then as now, Christian faith demanded a total realignment of self, and set a goal in which conventional achievement had little place, where material values are discarded and where service, not excellence, is the final criterion for judgement. But the caring professions, though essential, were not my choice. I was more concerned with processes and what was a bigger process than global materialism?

Instead of a place at theological college, I found myself working nights at Cadbury's factory in Bourneville. In retrospect perhaps this was more symbolically influential than I realised. John Cadbury opened a small store in Birmingham in 1824 but by the end of the century the business had become a model workplace with an extensive garden village. I was of an age and in a time when anything seemed possible. Was there a contemporary way of combining faith, work and social purpose? I'm pretty sure that none of these thoughts were at the front of my mind but as I nibbled my way through the nougat and mini-eggs in the small hours, who knows what ideas hatched?

It had been impossible to do sociology in the 1960s without quoting at every opportunity the well known writer who said, 'hitherto philosophers have interpreted the world, the point is to change it.' When those words were written the industrial revolution was in full swing. The mountains of production that we have come to take for granted were just small hills but their effect was already apparent. There were those who saw this as the start of humanity's triumph over its environment, the beginning of a process which would go ever onward and upward. There were also those who saw the process differently, as dehumanising individuals and destroying nature. The writer who expressed some of this was Karl Marx. Perhaps because of the failure of state communism in the late twentieth century it can be more clearly seen that one of the things that Marx did get right was the deep alienation that was being created between people, their work and the world that they were helping create.

His solution was primarily one that placed a great emphasis on the political process. His was an age of reform and revolution; 150 years ago people had great faith in politics. The great majority had not really seen big changes in their standard of living, and the consumer revolution was 100 years in the future. Today, particularly in the industrialized world, politics generally has a bad name, it has been tried and found wanting. By contrast, consumerism is still riding high. So if one wanted to change the world why not do it through the biggest idea around – shopping?

In the twenty-one years since Margaret Thatcher came to power and Traidcraft had begun to offer shopping with a conscience, the world's population has grown by about two billion – and remember it took about 2.1 million years to reach the first two billion. Are we undermining both human society and the foundations of life on earth? There is no doubt that for many, our efficiency-orientated, consumer society has delivered big benefits, but there are an increasing number of contradictions. The level of demand is constantly stimulated to be above the llevel of supply, new needs are created as soon as the old are satisfied. Luxury goods are re-classified as necessary consumer goods to make way for new luxury goods.

Christians in the 1970s were beginning to perceive that their faith must address these issues and I found much of my own concerns far more coherently set out in Hans Küng's *On Being A Christian* which was published in 1974. For me, this remains not only an intellectual guide which shows how one can be a Christian at the bar of reason, but also a practical guide to putting faith into practice. In one form or another, Traidcraft had large dollops of (often diluted) Küng stirred into its mix, one of the unforeseen results being a later affinity on a 'global ethic' with the present Labour government and a practical working relationship on these issues with the Department for International Development.

Most of the last fifty years has been a period of increasing prosperity in our society. Initially it was assumed that this would deliver increasing happiness. The idea is linked to the feeling that the capacity to consume is the essential proof of a successful life. The consumption of goods is a demonstration of status so if we want a better future, production and consumption must continually increase. Virtually all business subscribes to this assumption and implicitly targets growth and develops systems with growth as the objective. When we talk about consumer awareness, fair trading or social responsibility it is always in the context of resources flowing from a healthy and expanding commercial sector.

PROBLEMS WITH GROWTH

There are three big difficulties about this state of affairs. Firstly, in the western industrialised countries intangibles like happiness, fulfilment and social contentment have not noticeably increased with the increase in standards of living. The sense of community and personal worth and identity continues to be eroded.

The second big problem about growth is the continually widening gap between rich and poor countries, it has doubled in the last thirty years. For nearly 1,000 million people the problems of the world economy are only too apparent. They do not have sufficient food, they do not have clean water, and they do not have adequate shelter.

Thirdly, there is the impact of modern economies on our environment, local and global, which is giving great cause for concern. Global warming, pollution, population pressures, ozone depletion, deforestation, water and resource shortages – the list gets longer and longer. As the world discovers the joys of consumption, as people say 'I shop therefore I am', the very process by which we in the West have become affluent is being questioned by those who have been made affluent, and questioned at its deepest level. Can we go on like this? Is it sustainable? Is not the whole system flawed and ultimately self-destructive?

These were some of the ideas that were going into the concepts that underlay what I felt needed to be a radical and alternative trading organisation. The original concept behind Traidcraft was to set up a business in which the poor in developing countries would get a better price for their produce or work than they could through conventional business. It was to introduce equity into the trading process. It became clear that to do this effectively, many of the assumptions about how business operated would need to be questioned and alternatives found. In Traidcraft's formative years the idea of 'fair' trade, though present, was very much second to the idea of 'alternative' trade. Fairness has an implicit sense of balance and moderation. Being 'fair' was the social worker's approach to the economic system, being 'alternative' held out the possibility of radical change, of a new system that might be founded on principles of love and justice. Everybody knows what equity is – it is being equal. Fairness can be anything you want it to be. Being alternative was about changing the balance.

This happened at a time when the most radical political change of the century was taking place under Margaret Thatcher, the lady who successfully replaced the concept of equity in public service with efficiency. Not surprisingly, the new world order that Traidcraft subscribed to, held little attraction for free market economists. Ironically, Thatcherism stimulated the debate about business ethics and eventually led to the point where, eighteen years later, an incoming Labour government could espouse an ethical foreign policy and fair trade as electorally 'safe' platforms. Traidcraft played a part in this convergence, but there was a price to pay. There is now no recognised 'alternative' trading operation with significantly different values from those that many mainstream companies would adopt as part of their social 'licence to operate'. It may be the case that in moving from the margin to the mainstream the sharper, more cutting principles of a radical, Christian, social business have been carried away by the current or eroded by bumping into the debris that flows in the river of commercial life.

Throughout Traidcraft's twenty-one years its work has been interpreted in the context of the outworking of Christian faith. Many views have been presented and no doubt many more will continue to be formulated. Whether I personally agree with these or find them objectionable seems irrelevant. Providing Traidcraft as a context in which a Christian dialogue about these issues could take place, and the actual work undertaken by Traidcraft seems to me to be far more important than, as Marx might have said, merely interpreting what was happening.

Traidcraft was always intended to stimulate debate and inspire emulation in parallel fields. I hoped it could position itself as a beacon on the interface between spiritual and economic life. From this position I felt it should be exploring the three major themes of working, spending and saving. Concerning 'work', the business itself could aspire to be a home of best practice. Much effort in the early years went into staff participation, communication and trying to adopt good working practices and conditions. The extent to which they were achieved was more a reflection of the company's profitability and the experience of its managers – as opposed to our intentions! Exploring these issues was certainly a prime motivator for me in subsequently founding New Consumer, the business research charity that looked at the social and environmental ethics and programmes of major corporations, and tried to provide an objective basis for the emerging field of social accounting. It was encouraging to see Traidcraft following suit and developing an active role in this area which continues to the present day.

When it came to 'spending', Traidcraft itself was initially operating in the very narrow field of third world crafts. We rapidly branched out into food and beverages, recycled paper and clothing and 'study tours' – rather expensive and demanding visits for Traidcraft customers to our producers which nevertheless had an amazing impact and influence on many of the hundreds of people who went on them. I was keen to get into the sale of wholesome food, which, even in 1979, could be identified as an important issue of the future. One of the debates that ran for many years was the degree to which Traidcraft needed to have a 'fair trade' element in its foodstuffs. Initially I was keen to get into the market and build a 'whole food' position, but as the opportunity for Traidcraft to be a leader in this field passed I came round to the view that to maintain our 'beacon on a hill' approach we also had to show that our suppliers were also following progressive policies. Certainly a lot of the thinking that went into these issues emerged later in the founding of the Out of this World stores.

Traidcraft's first efforts to tackle the 'saving' side came in 1983 when we approached the Bank of England with the intention of setting up our own bank. Was it coincidence that shortly after that the financial regulation regime was considerably tightened up? Although rebuffed in this particular endeavour, Traidcraft did make a pioneering public share issue and over several years encouraged and supported the work that led to the establishment of Shared Interest, which has now attracted over £20 million in funds to help development through loan finance supporting initiatives in poorer countries.

As a catalyst, Traidcraft has, by most measures, been successful. But what of its core business? One of the difficulties that any Christian organisation has is how to judge its own effectiveness. Normal criteria of success are, for the Christian, turned on their head. Nevertheless, looking back at Traidcraft's birth, it is possible to see not only the achievements but also the numerous mistakes that were made and the risks that were taken. From my perspective, however, Christianity is a faith for the risk-taker. Christians can derive a strong sense of stewardship of resources, though until recently, this has been seen to apply only after the earth has been subdued. Yet against this we have an undoubtedly strong strand containing an almost complete rejection of material values. The focus and source of Christianity took the most immense 'risks' – confronting organised faith, business and authority at every turn. He took the ultimate step and had appeared to fail – but in that failure came a resurrection and redemption that still transforms people today.

But an organisation – as Traidcraft became – is not of itself responsive to a transforming message of love. In the early years, therefore, we set about building into the structures of the company a set of principles that sought to reflect how the staff and supporters defined a 'Christian' business. One of the interesting challenges was how to be inclusive, how to recognise that we were taking from other faiths, philosophies and programmes of political or business action, without losing a prime quality, the courage to fail in the service of love and justice. In Traidcraft's early days we set out a Basis of Faith and had a widespread consultation amongst staff, shareholders and suppliers to determine a set of Objectives, which later became the Foundation Principles. In other ways we tried to build into the organisation a set of faith-centred ethical values reinforcing them with a weekly worship meeting and an annual inspirational away-day. Much of what was set in place then was trying to 'fix' the values of those who had been involved in the start-up such as the staff and the more radical supporters of the parent Tearcraft.

At the same time we were trying to ensure that the ownership structure of the business would not be susceptible to an unfriendly takeover. This was perceived as particularly necessary when Traidcraft became a public company in 1984. With the benefit of hindsight, the structures that were put in place then were stultifying rather than protective. They empowered a small group of people, the trustees and directors, and effectively disenfranchised thousands of people who provided 95% of the capital. These people, the 'B' shareholders, were probably the antithesis of the share-trading, profit-maximising capitalist. They wanted Traidcraft to succeed as a radical Christian company. They would not have countenanced selling out to anyone who did not share these objectives.

Traidcraft, over the years, has been served by dozens of different people who have held non-executive positions of authority in its controlling bodies. There has been a substantial and sacrificial commitment of time by many, often in a purely voluntary capacity. Traidcraft, when compared with its contemporaries in the alternative trading movement, has been immensely successful thanks to the dedication of staff and customers – and more than a little support and tolerance from its suppliers. But Traidcraft has, by and large, failed to attract the innovative thinker and top-notch businessperson. Some might argue that this 'failure' has protected the company from losing its Christian identity but this is arguable. The majority shareholders, who have only received a cash dividend on their investment once in sixteen years, have had to accept a level of competence in the leadership of the business, starting with my own opening tenure, which would not be tolerated in the ordinary commercial world where the main providers of capital had a democratic voice. They have had no choice about this as Traidcraft's leadership and direction was set up initially to be largely self-selecting.

This is the area where I feel a particular sense of regret. In trying to protect the company against institutional capitalism, I gave little thought to providing a mechanism which would ensure a high quality of management and direction. The skills and enthusiasm needed for a start-up has to be supplemented and expanded as a business grows. In practice whatever is established in a constitution depends on the commitment and motivation of individuals in positions of authority to see that the spirit is maintained. Traidcraft remains as it was established in 1979, an organisation where a small number of people, fundamentally unaccountable to the majority, direct its affairs. This has been a strength at times, a weakness at others, but always an opportunity for change and improvement. In recent years much effort has gone into trying to find a way forward and the effective 'merging' of business and charity under common management in 1999 has been the major result so far, though it is too early to say with what effect.

A further challenge that Traidcraft faced at the end of the 1970s was how to reflect the voice of those it was seeking to support. We had ambitious plans for representation by producer groups, development agencies, our own staff, shareholders and customers. Perhaps this inclusive approach, never effectively carried out, contributed to the variable commercial and intellectual capacity of the Traidcraft board, but it is of particular regret that we never devised a way for the people making the goods we sold to have a say in the decision-making process. Now it is common practice amongst leading agencies to establish baseline positions and maintain impact assessments concerning new projects in developing countries. Traidcraft always has assumed it was 'doing good' but has never found the resources to truly evaluate its impact on the poor. After ten years of trading, the social accounts began this process but information and opinion is so often filtered through intermediary organisations, social and project workers and other international partners that a package rather than a true picture is inevitably the result.

There is one final strand amongst the many remaining that should be mentioned. Location. Traidcraft was not part of the London-Oxford axis that still defines the world of international development. Moving Tearcraft away from its original base in London was very much a conscious move to give a new organisation space to develop in its own way, and Traidcraft inherited this. Traidcraft has given jobs to hundreds of people in the North East and spawned several locally-based spin-off businesses. But it has undoubtedly paid a price, and not only in increased travel costs. Moving to Gateshead is not an obvious career move and in retrospect I can see that my insistence on a very low salary differential may also have put off the recruitment of essential new blood. Whilst we paid good rates for the majority of staff the salaries for senior positions were often 10–20% below their counterparts elsewhere. No matter how exciting and challenging the job a low-ish salary coupled with the possible uprooting of home and family was inevitably a major obstacle. Another feature in the North East is the macho business culture and whilst I believe we fought successfully against this for the most part Traidcraft nevertheless has only had one woman executive director on its board in its whole twenty-one years. The first of these issues has been addressed and salaries are now broadly comparable with similar organizations and it can only be a matter of time before women are a majority on the board![1]

Organisations mature much more quickly than individuals.

Traidcraft probably came of age with its public share issue in 1984 and went through a change of life in the mid-to-late 1990s with radical restructuring. Can Traidcraft now be said to be an 'elder' of the alternative trading movement? Does such a thing as corporate wisdom exist? Traidcraft certainly has an amazing fund of experience to draw on, a tradition that can either be a drag on progress or a keel providing stability and direction. This, as always, is the challenge that faces Traidcraft's staff and supporters. The company has resources and experience; it has goodwill and support from tens of thousands of customers and a significant national profile. The problems of poverty, of gross materialism, over-consumption and their consequences are worse today than when Traidcraft was founded. Traidcraft remains one of the few businesses that Christians of most traditions can identify with and to which they can make an unreserved commitment. Opportunity knocks.[2]

EDITORS' NOTES

1   Two of the four trustees are women.
2   We are grateful to Richard for providing these personal reflections over the genesis and development of Traidcraft. The views expressed are Richard's, and are not necessarily shared by the Trustees or the Directors.

Chapter Five

Traidcraft's Christian Basis and its Relationship with its Overseas Partners

Philip Angier

TWO REFERENCE POINTS

My chosen subject is to reflect upon Traidcraft's relationship with its overseas producers, and to do that I have chosen two reference points. The first draws upon biblical metaphor, the second draws upon Traidcraft's own Mission statement.

The Bible is full of metaphors. They are there to give us glimpses of the truth about God and our relationship with God. In Traidcraft we have been fond of contrasting two such metaphors – that of the *City on the Hill*[1] and that of *Salt*.[2] Which is the better metaphor for Traidcraft's work? Is it the city on the hill which draws those who support Traidcraft apart from the world to pursue a distinctive and elavated purpose? Or is it the salt which suggests that Traidcraft should be an agent of change, mixing and losing itself amongst the other ingredients in the pot and thereby affecting the taste of the whole. As my colleague, Graham Young, the founder director of Traidcraft Exchange, used to say: 'Salt is also a preservative so not only does it affect the taste but probably lengthens the shelf life of the food it is mixed with.'

Our debates sometimes became quite heated and were wont to force the issue as a *choice* between the two metaphors – if one picture is the right one for Traidcraft, the other one must be wrong. But, in truth, to treat them in this way is to create a false dichotomy.

Like so much of biblical teaching there is no definitive

answer – except to love God and love your neighbour. At different times we are called to live our lives in the manner of both the metaphors above. Loving God and loving our neighbour sometimes calls us to be like a city on a hill (calling people out from sin and pointing to the separateness of God's righteousness). At other times loving God and loving our neighbour calls us to be salt in the stew (worshipping and following the incarnate God who made friends with sinners and outcasts and proclaimed the Kingdom by living amongst us and sharing our messy and muddled lives).

The two metaphors sit side by side one another within the Sermon on the Mount. Perhaps common sense should have told us that they are intended as complementary, not competing, images. However, they do illustrate contrasting images of our engagement with the world as Christians, which can be confusing for us as individuals – and even more confusing for organisations seeking to walk the way of salvation.

That is why I take the risk of offering a third metaphor – a sort of 'third way'. The metaphor that I want to conjure with is that of *a Tabernacle on the Slopes*.

I think I probably need to explain this picture. First, imagine for yourself the city on the hill – high, beautiful but isolated, a long way and a hard climb from the valley where most of the population live. Then imagine that the salt metaphor can work in the same geography – the salt works where population lives, in the valley, mixing, savouring, disinfecting, preserving; not much salt is needed up on the hill. The first is distinctive, separate but reached by few. The second is in the midst of the populus, but quickly absorbed (and merging its identity with the greater whole).

The tabernacle on the slopes is set far enough apart to be clearly visible to the valley dwellers, but it is set low enough on the slopes so that more people can visit it.

I choose the tabernacle image from the Old Testament[3] because the tabernacle is a holy place imbued with spiritual significance, representational of God's dwelling place. It communicates the mystery, the holiness, the purity and the truth of God. It is set on the slopes because a prophetic message must visibly challenge the status quo, and call listeners 'apart' from the accepted norms of society (or its tolerated failures).

But the tabernacle is also mobile, it is a tent. God's truth may be unchanging but sin in society manifests itself in different ways at different times – greed, exploitation, corruption, conflict, oppression of women or caste, racism. The tabernacle metaphor allows us to reassess our priorities and to say 'we can move on from our stance against this issue, because many have heard what we had to say and social attitudes have changed. Now we see another social injustice becoming more prevalent and offending against God's Kingdom on earth. We will take our tabernacle and pitch it anew on the slopes on that side of the valley.'

I am fond of the metaphor because I think it helps us to see how we can embrace cultural relativism and remain faithful to God at the same time. But let us also beware – any metaphor is no more than a metaphor, and the Good Book also warns us against worshipping false idols.

My second reference point is *God's bias to the poor*. Traidcraft seeks to show a bias to the poor. We include it within our Mission Statement as one of our values:

> *Traidcraft is a Christian response to poverty. It strives to*
> * *Show a bias to the poor*
> * *Respect people and the environment*
> * *Be transparent and accountable*
> * *Show creativity and innovation*
> * *Be the best*

But with this declaration of intent comes an uncomfortable reality. If we are going to work out our discipleship with a bias to the poor, then *we must accept to make ourselves vulnerable*. The poor are by definition vulnerable. How else can we express solidarity with them without allowing ourselves to become vulnerable to some degree also?

God became incarnate amongst the poor, not the well to do. (Arguably since Joseph was a tradesman, God did not choose the bottom rung of the social ladder – but that is a debate for another day.) It is hard for us well-to-do professionals living in one of the world's richest societies to make *personal* choices about allowing vulnerability into our lives. It is harder still for

Traidcraft's Directors and Trustees to make *institutional* choices about how we allow a trading company and a charity to become 'vulnerable'. Would not that be a breach of our duty of care to shareholders or for the good stewardship of the assets and resources for which we are responsible?

But if we surround ourselves only with security and safety, I do not see how we can live out a bias to the poor

REFLECTIONS APPLIED

So I take the tabernacle metaphor and that uncomfortable commitment to live with a bias to the poor, and ask myself: what should these mean in practice for Traidcraft's relationships with its partners and producers?

Both the tabernacle metaphor and the bias to the poor suggest to me that there must be *a prophetic element in our calling*. The tabernacle reminds us of God's holiness and that to live in his presence means sometimes to be 'called apart'. A bias to the poor means taking sides – in the competitive market place it means taking sides with the 'losers', those who have not succeeded at accumulating wealth or exploiting economic advantage.

Today's political 'spin' suggests that in the great global economy, we are all 'winners' – that wealth creation is for all. Certainly there have been some gains – mass immunisation, reductions in infant mortality, improved literacy – especially in the last fifty years. But whilst health indicators may have improved, the wealth of the richest has grown disproportionately to the wealth of the poorest – and the average family in Africa is worse off in real terms than two decades ago, the gap between the richest and poorest on the planet has doubled in the last generation and now stands at 74:1! So the poor are losers in absolute and in relative terms, and that is a scandal.

Business is not conducted in a moral 'free trade zone' divorced from other social and ethical considerations. There is institutional sin and institutional grace in the world of commerce and trade, as in every other walk of life infected by or constructed by humans. We must witness against the sin, and proclaim the truth. This prophetic element should be evident in *our* corporate and individual behaviours, and be *shared* in the partnerships and alliances we make.

We are working *through* the market (in that sense we are the salt). However, we should be witnessing against unjust market structures, and unfair or selfish behaviour by market players be they middlemen, small businesses, corporations or multi-lateral organisations.

We should be celebrating those who succeed in bringing greater love and justice to commerce. We should be consistently calling upon those with economic advantage to adopt new values to behave in the market in new ways. Is it right that consumers are encouraged to view value only in terms of the cheapest price? As one of our Kenyan producers eloquently expresses it: 'A bargain is a bargain when both parties to the transaction leave feeling satisfied.' Traidcraft through its public share issues has encouraged investors to see a purchase of Traidcraft shares as an investment in someone else's future. The term 'fat-cat salaries' sticks because of the manifest greed of some Directors' pay. Traidcraft seeks in its remuneration policy to ask 'when is enough, enough?'

We should and do choose as our partners those who are manifestly concerned to bring about social change and social justice.

And if we believe that a bias to the poor affects our lives and our organisational thinking, and encourages us to accept vulnerability as part of our calling, then we must look for and expect some of those same qualities in those with whom we choose to make partnerships.

All of this is saying that there is a spiritual dimension to development – and our partnerships recognise and express this.

What then about *cross-cultural communication*? We must be honest about our roots and our grounding in faith. To be a 'faith-based' organisation is (as Chris Sugden, Chair of the Traidcraft Foundation says) not the same as to be 'faith promoting'. But equally, to be a 'faith based' organisation means that we should not be 'faith hiding', let alone 'faith denying'. Traidcraft is called to carry the cross proudly.

Some partners or producers may want to exploit the altruism that is born out of our Christian heart; others may find it difficult to accept our faith basis without suspecting an agenda of cultural imperialism. I believe that we can avoid both of these pitfalls if we remain honest to our values and consistent in our behaviour. But sometimes such honesty may work against short term economic advantage or expediency.

More importantly *we must practise how to listen*. This again stems from our commitment to a 'bias to the poor'. Most often our partners and producers are much closer to the poor and *de facto* a lot more vulnerable than us. Fighting poverty is not concerned only with poverty as economically measured. It means also addressing the non-economic signs of poverty (access to health and education, gender equity, right to self-determination). We can only understand these if we listen to the voices of the poor.

This is not easy for us to do. We are in a power relationship where our views (or what our partners perceive to be our views) hold disproportionate sway. We are mostly white, mostly middle class, mostly university educated. We come with – and communicate – all the baggage of the colonial over-class. And because English is the widely accepted language of business we expect to communicate in our first language, not that of our partners.

Traidcraft must enable those in immediate dialogue with partners to develop the capacity to listen – and to record and to feedback. We must try to make sure that dialogue takes place in contexts where our own views and values are not determining the agenda. Traidcraft's leaders and directors, as holders of corporate strategy and guardians of its mission *must practise listening* – not just introspective dialogue.

One way in which Traidcraft has tried to systematise its learning from and listening to feedback from stakeholders is through its social accounting process. The box on the page following describes briefly what this process involves.

These reflections challenge Traidcraft to consider how much attention it presently gives to sharing our Christian values with those staff members who work for us overseas. How often do we reflect together why we hold the values we do, and how we want the staff representing Traidcraft to communicate them in our dealings with partners? If these values are at the root of our purpose and being, we should not simply leave it up to each

---

Social Accounting

Traidcraft has been a pioneer of Social Accounting in the UK. It published its first independently audited Social Accounts in 1993. Traidcraft began down the path of social accounting for three reasons:

- in order to give an account against its stated mission and goals to its Foundation Trustees;

- in order communicate openly and transparently with its stakeholders; and

- in order to be a learning organisation – allowing learning from past successes and failures to strengthen future operations.

The social accounting method involves systematically collecting and reporting the voices and views of stakeholders including Traidcraft's producers and partners, through questionnaires, interviews and focus groups.

---

staff member to discern her/his own answer to these questions

I do not wish to be misunderstood. I am not implying that I think that Traidcraft has got it all horribly wrong. I am not saying that I consider our staff to be insensitive, still less unprofessional in what they do. I reflect simply that Traidcraft puts much more emphasis in their job training on the measurables of what they do than on the values by which they live and work – and by default we leave them to work out more of the values basis for themselves.

What about when we are *dealing with non-Christian partners* (or potential partners) overseas?

Traidcraft recognises a shared commitment to the poor in those of other creeds and none. In many parts of the world the local church is stronger (much stronger) than in the UK. In some parts of the world Christians are an oppressed minority. At times Traidcraft may find itself working alongside institutions unsympathetic to these Christian minorities.

In my opinion, that an oppressed minority is Christian is no greater nor no lesser reason for standing up for their rights. Dalits, or East Timorese, or women, or any other group who are oppressed are all equally deserving of solidarity and support. If we are dealing with a partner whose faith basis is not Christian, we should not be arrogant about our faith, but we should remain consistent to our values, 'faith-based' not faith-promoting'.

CONCLUDING THOUGHTS

How should Traidcraft's basis of faith best be expressed in our dealings with producers and partners? A communiqué from the recent conference of African church leaders meeting leaders from the World Bank begins with the words of Jesus quoting Isaiah: 'The Spirit of the Lord has anointed me to preach Good News to the poor.'[4]

Traidcraft's calling is to *do* good news *with* the poor, and to *listen* to the voices of the poor in order to hear what is 'good news' in their terms.

NOTES

1   Matthew 5:14.
2   Matthew 5:13.
3   Exodus 33–34.
4   Luke 4:18; Isaiah 61:1. See Communiqué from World Bank and Council of Anglican Provinces of Africa on alleviating poverty in Africa, *Transformation*, October 2000, Vol. 17 No. 4, and Belshaw, Deryke; Calderisi, Robert and Sugden, Chris, *Faith in Development: Possibilities for Partnership between the World Bank and the Churches of Africa* (Oxford: Regnum, and Washington: World Bank, 2001).

Chapter Six

Traidcraft and its Staff

Yvonne Dare

> It may be a cliché that people are an organisation's greatest
> asset, but no organisation exists without them and nothing is
> achieved except through people. Therefore personnel practices
> go to the heart of the organisation and potentially have a role in
> every facet of its activities.[1]

Few would probably argue against the premise that the pivotal
role which staff play in any commercial enterprise is a major
determinant of the success or failure of that organisation.
Acknowledgment of that fact has been a catalyst for the development and implementation of new employment legislation in
the UK which, in recognition of the important contribution
made by employees to the economy, has resulted in the introduction of laws to ensure improved and more equitable working
practices.

In considering how the Christian basis of Traidcraft can best
be expressed in relation to its staff we will reflect on the follow-
ing three areas:
Sacred or secular? – discerning the difference
Precept or practice? – how can we express God's love?
Safety or sacrifice? – paying the price.

SACRED OR SECULAR?

Reflecting on the impact of Christian influence on the working
practices and relationships which emerged in Traidcraft's early
days, Richard Adams comments

> A religious statement set out our basis of faith in the original
> deed of trust for Traidcraft... All trustees had to 'affirm' this

document; directors and senior staff had to be 'in sympathy'...
But whatever was included constitutionally, it was the staff who
reflected the underlying ethos of the business.[2]

In 1979, when Traidcraft commenced, all of the founding
employees who had moved across from Tearcraft to form the
new company were professing Christians. Early employment
recruitment was specifically targeted at the Christian community, with job vacancies being advertised virtually exclusively
in churches in the local area.

As both Traidcraft plc and Traidcraft Exchange developed,
so the need for specialist skills and knowledge increased. It
soon became apparent that these were not always readily available in those seeking employment in the local Christian community or those willing to relocate to the north-east of England.
A pragmatic approach has thus proved necessary in interpreta-
tion of the requirement for senior staff to be 'in sympathy' with
the deed of trust in order to ensure that staff with the appropriate
levels of skills and experience are recruited and appointed to
senior posts in the organisation.

There have been occasions in the recruitment process itself
when interviewees have not felt comfortable with the Christian
basis of the company. At least one applicant for a senior position decided not to proceed to second interview because he/she
did not feel comfortable with the Christian ethos. In the recruitment and selection process particular care is taken to ensure that
staff appointed to positions where they are required to represent
the organisation externally are competent at, and feel comfortable with, articulating the nature and relevance of the Christian
basis of Traidcraft when appropriate to do so. The need for
senior staff to fulfill a similar role internally is perhaps something that should be more overtly acknowledged.

From its inception, Traidcraft has purported to reflect its
Christian basis in its dealings with people, including its staff.
The original Foundation Principles included reference to the
promotion of 'employment with improved conditions' which
was defined as meaning employment that met the majority of
eleven stated criteria related to reward, job suitability, opportunities for personal development through training, the provision

of adequate, appropriate resources, and a pleasant and safe working environment. The current Foundation Principles (see Appendix Two) and the Mission Statement remind us that we continue to be 'challenged by Jesus to be both a lamp on a stand (to give light to society around) and to be yeast in the dough (being closely involved in society).' Part of the ongoing responsibility of Traidcraft is to discover how to be ever more faithful to this calling.

Such aspirations are bold. For an organisation to declare them publicly leaves it open to challenge both from within the organisation and externally. Twenty-one years after Traidcraft's inception, consideration needs to be given to whether the experience of the past confirms that the Christian basis of the organisation has resulted in an approach to staff and to the formulation of personnel policies and procedures which differ significantly from those prevailing in any other commercial enterprise which seeks to implement best practice in its human resources policies and practice. If those claims can be substantiated, it is important that the manner of their outworking in practice and their relevance for the Traidcraft of the twenty-first century are identified, evaluated and developed for the benefit of those who currently work for Traidcraft as well as those who will do so in the future, in order that the mission of Traidcraft to alleviate poverty might be furthered.

We need also to consider whether any discernible distinction can be drawn between a sacred or secular approach to human resource issues. If so, are any particular resultant challenges, constraints or tensions placed upon the organisation by its Christian basis?

Perhaps such a question is best addressed by those in Traidcraft who do not profess a personal Christian faith. One such member of staff, retiring recently after a number of years with the organization, was asked whether from her experience she believed that the Christian basis of Traidcraft had made it different from other companies. If so, could she describe the manner in which that difference had been expressed? She responded that she believed that the values emanating from Traidcraft's Christian basis (values which she held dear although she could not ascribe personally to the faith which they represent) had provided a tangible support and structure for staff, which was manifested in a caring, listening, friendly environment, which she described in terms of family life. She had not experienced this to such a high degree in other companies for which she had worked. She attributed this directly to the organisation's Christian basis.

It may be comparatively easy to attribute the difference defined by that former member of staff to an individual personal faith. For example, a senior manager seeking to live out a commitment to Christ on a daily basis in the work-place through a 'caring, listening, friendly' response to others does not so much represent a conscious adherence to a policy which is written down, but rather reflects the practical expression of a personal spiritual motivation. However, in terms of the faith-base of the organisation, it may well best be reflected in the corporate culture of Traidcraft.

A study of the management of Christian service organisations in the United States of America notes that many of the questions most frequently addressed to staff, volunteers, donors and observers of those organisations show a high proportion seeking to discover what made an organisation 'Christian'. Drawing on his own experience, the author, Thomas H. Jeavons, concludes that

> The key elements for shaping their character as Christian are two: the personal characteristics and commitments of their staff, especially in relation to their faith commitments; and the manner in which the staff are managed and led to maintain a Christian 'organizational culture'. These two factors are, in fact, inextricably woven together because it may be that the most important thing the managers and leaders do is choose and support the staff to develop that culture.[3]

Traidcraft's mission statement asserts that, it is 'a *Christian* response to poverty'. If this claim is true, then the nurture and promotion of what Thomas H. Jeavons describes as 'ultimate' or moral values will be seen on a day to day basis in the decisions and actions of the organisation. It follows that the expression of Traidcraft's spiritual values in its policies and actions should best distinguish it from other organisations which do not claim the same values-base.

There may be a variety of ways to 'fight poverty through trade'. The fact that Traidcraft has chosen to do so, and to witness that it has done so, as a conscious response to its Christian basis, should inevitably result in approaches and practices which are recognisably different from organisations which do not share the same spiritual motivation.

Respecting and nurturing the ethos arising from those fundamentally Christian values (defending the faith) is costly for both individuals and organisations. It makes demands on both the organisation and individuals in terms of time, energy and commitment, and puts them in a place of vulnerability.

The corporate faith-base of Traidcraft will, however, have little impact unless it is intrinsic in the daily life of the organisation, permeating all the activities of the decision-makers in Traidcraft, acting as salt and light, influencing every decision, underpinning every strategy, and reflected in every response and relationship.

PRECEPT OR PRACTICE?

How should Traidcraft's Christian basis *best* be expressed in relation to staff? Fundamental to the human resources management function of any organisation claiming a Christian faith-base should be a dual mission which embodies moral and spiritual values, while providing opportunities for practical service to its employees.

Valuing people consists not only in providing a 'caring, friendly environment' in which they can work, giving due attention to their health and safety in the workplace, providing them with a job which is suited to their skills, knowledge and capabilities, and developing them through training and learning opportunities, but also in taking a holistic view of them, recognising the spiritual dimension of their lives, and ensuring that the workplace is an area where that aspect of their lives can also be nurtured and developed.

In identifying some of the spiritual gifts which were available through the Holy Spirit to the early church for the building up of the body of Christ, the Apostle Paul concludes

And now I will show you the best way of all ... make love your aim.[4]

Since Traidcraft's Christian basis derives from the very essence and nature of God, which the Apostle John describes as 'love',[5] it is imperative that such love, as demonstrated in the life and teaching of God incarnate, should be the hallmark of Traidcraft's relationship with its staff and the touchstone against which the organisation's human resource strategy and policies are formulated. This must be the outstanding feature which distinguishes any organisation claiming a Christian faith-base from others in the commercial and charity world which make no such claim.

In the final discourse with the disciples prior to his crucifixion, Jesus uses the metaphor of himself as the vine and his followers as the branches to illustrate how spiritual fruitfulness provides the tangible evidence of true discipleship in his followers after his return to the Father. He gives the explicit command that they should demonstrate the same love for one another as he has shown for them. The Apostle John returns to this theme in his first letter, exhorting the early church:

... let us love one another, for love comes from God. Everyone who loves has been born of God, because God is love. Whoever does not love does not know God, because God is love.[6]

Taking its cue from this, the Traidcraft Foundation Principles (revised 1999) (see Appendix Two) remind us that we are called upon 'To express an inclusive community of purpose and relationships, acknowledging the Christian precept of love by putting the interests of others before one's own.'

So, let us consider briefly some of the ways in which Traidcraft may seek to ensure that the Christian precept of love is revealed in practice in relation to its staff.

The New Testament emphasises the need for an integration of faith and works. In his eschatalogical teaching immediately preceding his arrest and crucifixion, recorded in St Matthew's Gospel,[7] Jesus reminds his disciples that the most tangible expression of their faith will be the care and service demonstrated to those who are most vulnerable or needy. If Traidcraft is to be effective in demonstrating the faith on which it is founded it must seek to adopt and foster an ethos which reflects the nature of him who

> ... being in the very nature of God, did not consider equality with God something to be grasped, but made himself nothing, assuming the nature of a slave.[8]

Reflecting on the Christian motivation which resulted in the formation of Traidcraft, Richard Adams draws a distinction between the current obsession for the search for 'excellence' in the business world, with its focus on materialism and acquisitiveness coupled with a drive for personal achievement, and the biblical concept of servanthood with its roots in social justice and sacrifice. He reminds us that

> Jesus gives us a personal mission statement which demands a total realignment of ourselves, a goal in which conventional achievement has no place, where material values are discarded and where service, not excellence, is the final criterion for judgement.[9]

The gospel narrative challenges Christians to demonstrate love visibly in their daily lives by serving their neighbours and each other, by caring for the poor, the widows, and the orphans, and by assisting 'the least of the brethren' (Matt. 20:26–27; Lk. 10:25–37; Gal. 5:13; Phil. 2:5–18). Nowhere should this response be more apparent in an organisation which claims a Christian basis for its work than in its dealings with staff and all its other stakeholders. The practical outworking of that faith in a corporate setting should stand as a witness, both to that faith and to the command of the one who instigated it when he instructed his followers to

> Let your light shine before men, that they may see your good deeds and praise your Father in heaven.[10]

Therefore, if the faith basis is real and relevant, it must also be apparent in the policies and practices of the organisation and play a vital role in witnessing for Christ.

Christ commands, rather than just encourages, his followers to let their light shine (the Greek verb is in the imperative), so that the work which they do in his name will be a testimony to God's love. The prominent position of the *'city set on a hill'* will inevitably mean that it is there for all to see, open to scrutiny both from within and outside the organisation, and rightly so. The profession of faith which it makes must, therefore, be totally credible.

Jeavons challenges organisations to consider that

[If they] use the term 'Christian' in their name or the explanation for what they do, they have a special obligation to make sure the way they perform that service (and operate more generally) reflects Christian ideals and beliefs, because it will be seen as – and ought to make – a statement about their faith.[11]

At the heart of the Christian gospel is the assertion that people matter – the extent of their value to God having been expressed in the sacrifice of his own Son for their redemption – and the way that a Christian employer treats the staff working for them should reflect the value that Christ places on individuals. The consistent message of the New Testament is that Christ always had time for individuals, that he was prepared to expend time and energy to bring out the best – to release the potential – in them, that he showed infinite patience in dealing with them, that he recognised their needs, and that he was prepared to listen to them and share in their experiences. That is the standard against which Traidcraft has to measure the effectiveness of its personnel practices.

Seeking to make 'love our aim' will require a recognition of the infinite value of all human beings, which will include acknowledging the worth of each individual member of staff in the organisation. It will involve a willingness to try and see each individual staff member through God's eyes rather than human eyes, to value them for who they are, and for the potential which lies within them. It means acknowledging that they are created in God's image, of infinite value and have a place in God's plan. Christ's parable of the sheep and goats recorded in Matthew 25 and the subsequent lesson which he draws from it, challenges the Christian community to recognise that their opportunities to express their love for him will be presented in the human interfaces which confront them on a daily basis. They will be judged according to their responsiveness to the needs with which they are presented.

The advent of the technological age may, on occasion, have

put disproportionate emphasis on the importance of technical resources to the neglect or detriment of human resources. But sometimes companies have discovered to their cost that technology can be subject to failure. Technology does not have the capacity for spontaneous innovative creative responses to problems which human resources can provide. This was graphically illustrated in Traidcraft during the peak selling period leading up to Christmas 1999 when serious problems with the implementation of a new computer system resulted in major operational problems which threatened the viability of the business. Although the technical resources failed and were unable to provide the service which the business required at that time, the human ones did not. On the contrary, staff at all levels in the organisation showed their flexibility, resourcefulness, energy and commitment to Traidcraft's mission. They provided practical solutions, often at personal expense, to maintain the best level of customer service which was humanly possible and to minimise the negative impact on the organisation's fight against poverty. The frustrations and disappointment caused by the failure of systems were as keenly felt and shared by members of the operational staff as by the executive team.

Traidcraft's commitment to following the way of love in its dealings with staff will be manifest in an holistic approach to those individuals who work for it, as part of a recognition of the spiritual needs of all its stakeholders and of the organisation in general.

Just as prayer and worship are integral to the spiritual development of the individual Christian, so they have a vital role to play in the development of organisations which claim an identity with Christ. A weekly worship session lasting between twenty and thirty minutes, which is open to all staff, has been integral to Traidcraft's working week since its earliest days. It currently provides an opportunity for personal reflection and corporate prayer for both individuals and work-related or personal situations at the beginning of the week. It is led on a voluntary basis by members of staff from all levels in the organisation who regularly attend. They come from a variety of Christian denominations. Discussion has taken place from time to time on whether it is appropriate for the worship session to continue to be held during work time. Some Christians have felt that it was not appropriate for them to attend while their non-Christian colleagues continued working.

The fact that each Traidcraft board meeting and the meetings of the Trustees commence with a period of prayer and reflection is indicative of the importance that those who lead and manage the organisation place upon the guidance of God in its decision-making, the outcome of which inevitably has an impact upon staff.

In taking account of the holistic needs of its staff, Traidcraft has a duty to accept its responsibility for seeking to enable those who work for the organisation to recognise the need for balance in their lives, in order that they might experience the 'life in all its fulness' which is exclusively available in Christ.[12] The chief executive of one of the organisations which Jeavons studied described his primary tasks as

> ... setting a tone, establishing expectations about values, ethics, and integrity in our work; and setting priorities for how we will work. My priorities are God first, family second, and then work; and I want those priorities to pervade the organisation... It is crucial for the executive to model the behaviour he wants to see in an organisation.[13]

His staff affirm that he sets an example by his own behaviour which is entirely consistent with those tasks and the objective to be an exemplar. He also reinforces them with policy by, for example, making the taking of holiday leave mandatory for all staff and establishing training programmes for supervisory staff to enable them to learn effective delegation.

The corporate culture of an organisation will inevitably influence, and may even constrain, the manner and scope of the personnel function within it. An examination of the role of personnel practitioners[14] suggests that the indicators for determining whether an organisation has a positive or negative culture include:

- management style – whether employees are managed by instruction and control or by consultation and personal development;
- employees – whether they are they valued and if so, how it is

expressed;
- profit – whether employees are conscious of it, and its relevance or importance;
- business objectives – whether employees identify with them;
- ethics – whether ethics are important and if so, how it is obvious;
- risks – the consequences of making a mistake; and
- pay – whether it is fixed or linked to performance, grading or 'merit'.

The evidence of Jeavons' study of North American Christian service organisations suggests that the corporate culture of what were deemed to be the most successful of those organisations which he studied had been, and continued to be, strongly influenced by the priority which their chief executives gave to articulating and modelling the mission and values which they wished to see operative in their organisations. Pivotal to the success in demonstrating its values-base in a way which is both meaningful and credible to the staff of any organisation claiming a Christian basis is the vitally important roles which both executive and non-executive directors must fulfil in providing sound leadership and management based on those values, together with a consistent example of them lived out on a daily basis in their own personal lives. Such evidence adds strong support to the crucial role played in the recruitment and selection of appropriate executives and other senior staff, if the Christian basis of an organisation is to continue to be espoused and exemplified.

The emergent culture of an organisation will undoubtedly be a good indicator of the effective outworking of the values upon on which it is based.

SAFETY OR SACRIFICE

In an organisation which professes a Christian basis, the recognition of staff as its most precious resource should result in treatment which supports that recognition and in a working relationship with them which reflects it. However, that kind of recognition will inevitably create tensions in an environment of competing priorities.

In November 1980 when Traidcraft's predominantly Christian staff establishment still numbered less than twenty, the Finance Director, Brian Hutchins, commenting on the high proportion of those staff who were presenting with a variety of personal problems on which they sought counselling from senior staff, observed that the company seemed to be 'turning into a social work department'. The Traidcraft ethos has resulted in the continued provision of what the then Education Adviser, Jan Simmonds, described at the time as 'an atmosphere ... where people don't feel threatened, where they can open up because they know they will find support.'[15] The practical outworking of Traidcraft's Christian basis has continued to be revealed in a 'caring' work environment which is sensitive to and supportive of staff. The Human Resources department and some senior staff members are called upon to provide confidential counselling or referral to professional bodies on a wide range of staff problems related both to work and private life.

The introduction of an 'open door policy' which ensures that the Director of Human Resources is generally accessible to staff at the times which they regard as urgent, rather than a time which the diary indicates is preferable from a work-load viewpoint, has contributed to pressures to meet deadlines and difficulties in maintaining a reasonable work-load. But that policy continues because it is perceived as part of a Christian response to staff. On occasions it has also proved necessary for immediate practical implementation of a policy before that policy has been formally formulated or agreed.

Seeking to recognise the worth of each individual staff member in an organisation also creates a responsibility to endeavour to provide those employees with opportunities for their personal and career development. In a Christian organisation this may be regarded as helping them to 'become mature, attaining to the whole measure of the fulness of Christ',[16] to assist them in identifying the God-given gifts and abilities which they have and to look for opportunities to develop them and to help them to progress towards their full potential.

In addition to helping staff to discover and develop those aptitudes and abilities which are necessary to enable them to fulfil the requirements of their daily work, the Christian organisation may well consider whether it has a simultaneous role in enabling them to recognise the importance which the Christian faith also places upon 'being' as opposed to 'doing'.

As an employer seeking to make love its aim, Traidcraft has an important role to play in providing a working environment and the personal development opportunities necessary to enable staff to reach their full potential and hopefully, as a by-product, to find fulfilment in their job.

In practical terms, this means seeking to ensure that each individual member of staff has a job which is necessary, stretching, challenging and suited to their skills. This inevitably presents challenges to any organisation, and particularly to those seeking to continue their effectiveness in a changing business environment or a period of change management. For example, in 1996 Traidcraft plc underwent major organisational restructuring which indicated the need for a radical reduction in staffing levels. The painful, but vitally important, decision was taken to make one-third of the staff redundant since the need for their particular jobs had disappeared in the new business structure. This challenged us to expand our understanding of what was compatible with the Christian love to which Traidcraft aspires.

Each of the decisions which has resulted in staff losing their jobs, for whatever reason, in either Traidcraft plc or Traidcraft Exchange throughout the organisation's twenty-one years of existence has been made after much agonising and at the expense of a great deal of mental and emotional stress by those responsible for the decisions. During those difficult periods the compatibility of such decisions with the Christian principles of love which Traidcraft espouses were called into question by some staff and supporters, representative of both those who did and did not profess a Christian faith.

On some occasions during Traidcraft's recent history the organisation has felt compelled to preserve the dignity of those staff for whom it could no longer continue to provide a job which fulfilled those criteria, by helping them to recognise the need for them to move into more appropriate employment outside Traidcraft, and by assisting them to prepare for and make that move. In an organisation which has traditionally enjoyed a very low staff turnover, there have been a few staff, both among those who have left Traidcraft and those who have remained, who have found it difficult to come to terms with the recognition that in these decisions Traidcraft has demonstrated its integrity and Christian love. Traidcraft has sought to reflect its values-base by the level of its investment in time and financial resources to provide appropriate counselling and training for those involved and the use of its best efforts to try and assist those affected to find more suitable employment outside of Traidcraft. There have inevitably also been times when tensions have been created by the struggle to balance those requirements against financial constraints (for example, for training, etc.) and the limited opportunities for career progression which the organisation has been able to provide in reality.

Throughout its history, Traidcraft has taken positive steps towards the empowerment of its staff at all levels in the organisation. At times this may well have meant consciously putting the organisation in a situation of potential risk and vulnerability since it has involved giving staff a voice, and enabling them to participate in, and have an influence upon, the decision-making processes of the organisation.

A commitment to communication and consultation with staff on issues pertinent to them has sometimes been the cause of some frustration when it has resulted in practical terms in slowing change or protracting the implementation of new policies. But invariably the frustration has proved worthwhile and the value of staff involvement has been recognised in the outcome.

Since its inception, provision has been made under the Traidcraft plc Articles of Association for two staff members to be elected to the board of directors from among their number. Consideration is currently being given to whether this continues to be an appropriate form of staff representation. There has also been some anxiety expressed through the Staff Association over a perception that the value placed upon the human resource function in the organisation might be diminishing with the shift from executive to senior management status of the head of that function over recent years. The willingness of Traidcraft management to engage in debate and to consult fully with staff on these issues is an indication of its ongoing commitment to serve those who work for it in the best way possible.

To be an effective Christian witness to its staff Traidcraft must continue to aspire to be, and work towards being, transparent and accountable in its dealings with them. In an analysis of the UK's most successful companies a number of those researched highlighted the importance of integrity towards their employees as being an important contributing factor in their company's success, and the study found that 'A low employee perception of the company's fairness tends to be associated with a poor opinion of top management.'[17] This includes making an investment of time to work with, as well as for, staff. It involves opening ourselves to scrutiny, exposing the organisation to the vulnerability resulting from differing perceptions and expectations of the influence of our Christian basis, both from within and outside the organisation.

A LAST WORD

We started out by asking whether Traidcraft is different from any other commercial enterprise which seeks to implement best practice in its human resources policies and practice. If it is, or if it aspires to be, a word of caution – there is a price to be paid. The commitment to follow the one who turned employment strategies on their heads and to 'make love our aim' as an expression of Traidcraft's Christian basis in relation to staff is costly, it calls for tough decisions, it involves sacrifice and leads to cross-bearing – but in the context of our Traidcraft's mission it is the only way!

NOTES

1   Malcolm Martin and Tricia Jackson, *Personnel Practice* (Trowbridge: Cromwell Press, 1997), p. 6.
2   Richard Adams, *Who Profits?* (Oxford: Lion, 1989), p. 157.
3   Thomas H. Jeavons *When the Bottom line is Faithfulness* (Bloomington: Indiana University Press, 1994), p. 81.
4   1 Corinthians 12:31; 14:1.
5   1 John 4:8.

6   1 John 4:7–8 (NIV).

7   Matthew 25:31–46 (NIV).

8   Philippians 2:6–7 (NIV).

9   Adams, *Who Profits?*, p. 50.

10   Matthew 5:16 NIV.

11   Jeavons, *When the Bottom Line is Faithfulness*, p. 48.

12   John 10:10.

13   Jeavons, *When the Bottom Line is Faithfulness*, p. 188.

14   Martin and Jackson, *Personnel Practice*, p. 13.

15   Adams, *Who Profits?*, p. 77.

16   Ephesians 4:13 (NIV).

17   Walter Goldsmith and David Clutterbuck, *The Winning Streak* (Harmondsworth: Penguin, 1985), p. 160.

Chapter Seven

Traidcraft and its Fair Traders

Campbell Grant

To define Traidcraft as a legal entity, with some paid staff, some shareholders, and a history read as a set of returns to Companies House, is too limiting. A rounded picture of Traidcraft can only be seen if the organisational boundary is drawn to include the 5000 or so Fair Traders – those direct selling agents, or representatives, who buy from Traidcraft at a discount to sell on to end consumers in locations all over the UK. Fair Traders are not external agents who interact with a Traidcraft whose identity is set by another group (such as the Traidcraft Board). Rather, they *are* Traidcraft – or at least a part of it. We might speak of 'the Traidcraft community' as being the interactions of 'Traidcraft the company' – that is the formal part in Gateshead that Companies House staff see as Traidcraft – with its dispersed informal members: Fair Traders (and shareholders and donors and other categories of members, too).

Many Fair Traders are Christian, and their faith is integral to how they see Traidcraft. But the nature of the Christian basis to the Traidcraft community can be seen in many ways. At one end of the spectrum is a minimalist view that would see the functioning of the processes that are Traidcraft-in-operation as having no spiritual dimension at all. In this view the Christian basis is a purely motivational factor: some people (many Fair Traders, the founders of Traidcraft, a proportion of staff, etc.) chose or choose to be committed to Traidcraft because of a personal Christian faith. (The founders happen to have had the opportunity to stick a 'basis of faith' to the organisation – like an irrelevant label on a suitcase reminding us of ports others visited long ago but to which we will never go.) This is an approach to the organisation of Traidcraft that sees it in mechanistic (or at least secular) terms – with faith being a private and personal matter.

At the other end of the spectrum is the view that the Christian basis is as much a part of what Traidcraft *is* as is breath to a living body. In this view Traidcraft is not a trading/development organisation which happens to have been set up by Christians and stamped with 'their' label – as though it were a group of 'Christians responding to poverty' (as one legitimately can through Oxfam or ActionAid), but just doing their own thing. Rather it is a 'Christian response to poverty' – as Traidcraft's values statement proclaims. In this sense Traidcraft's representatives are a dispersed community of radical Christians seeking to respond to the 'peace and justice' imperative of the gospel in a distinctively Christian way. The Traidcraft company is merely the localised part of this radical community.

Is the role of the Traidcraft community in responding to the issues around 'Markets, Fair Trade and the Kingdom of God' to be a 'best practice' development organisation whose members are personally motivated by Christian faith? Or is the Traidcraft community a picture of what redemption means in *social* terms (and is a Traidcraft without a Christian basis an oxymoron)? These are the key questions and are not just of academic interest: our answers will guide Traidcraft's future.

ORIGINS AND POSSIBLE FUTURES

Many Fair Traders became Fair Traders because Traidcraft was (is?) a Christian organisation offering Christians (and all people of goodwill, of course) an opportunity to respond to the injustices of world trade, and to take practical action as part of their Christian discipleship. (There are other options – such as volunteering for Oxfam. Whilst some may do both, some Fair Traders have consciously chosen to be a Fair Trader precisely because it includes the Christian dimension.)

If the people who are Traidcraft are only the 100-plus people in a Gateshead office we would be as able to switch the direction of Traidcraft (or reinvent it) as rapidly as any other small company – bearing in mind that a company without customers is nothing. But if Fair Traders are part of Traidcraft, and if there are 30 fair traders for every staff member (and there are more), then the army of Fair Traders provides a kind of reservoir of collective understanding of what Traidcraft *is*. To describe it in terms of inertia has negative connotations – but the notion that paid staff (or board members, for that matter) *could not* 'switch off' the Christian basis of Traidcraft (even if they wished to) is important. Our history does not define our future, but the collective memory of Fair Traders about what it means to be a Christian organisation is a strong determinant.

What could be is not the only question. We must also ask what *should be*. If organisational integrity is to mean keeping faith with those whose time, energy and investments have enabled Traidcraft to grow over twenty-one years, then understanding and developing the Christian basis is the way forward, not marginalising and diminishing it.

SECULARISATION: FORCES FOR AND AGAINST

What is the fate of faith-based organisations in a post-modern world? Some would argue that to be faith-based is by definition to occupy a niche, and that to be mainstream demands that the faith-base should become history. Dr Barnardo's is the paradigm: what began as a faith-based organisation became a market leader by growing up and leaving home. This does not imply any watering down of values, but it draws a clear distinction between a faith-base and a values-base, and seeks to retain the values while sitting loose to (and ultimately discarding) the faith-base. That could be a legitimate choice for the Traidcraft community, but we should remember that adage that 'only dead fish go with the flow.'

If the Kingdom of God is a 'here and now' thing, then Christian faith is about the public and the political, not just private piety (as it might be if 'pie in the sky when you die' were all that faith meant). The privatisation of religion has a long history in western culture and has many roots (including, perhaps, the ugliness of the church as the world's first transnational corporation). That stifling 'not-in-front-of-the-children' environment has sometimes been met with compliance, or – and often appropriately – by a kind of assimilation. (Christians in politics may do more good in mainstream parties than in faith-based pressure groups.) But the reaction to the forces of privatisation can rightly include celebrating the place of distinctively Christian contributions to our common life. Traidcraft has, in a small way, reclaimed parts of a secular marketplace and demonstrated the integral connection of faith and trade. Many Fair Traders have joined Traidcraft precisely because it does offer a practical outworking of faith in an arena from which the church has been in retreat.

That faith is part of everyday life, not just a private hobby for those who are so minded, has not needed to be discovered in much of the world: it was never forgotten. That it is being rediscovered in the West can be seen in many quarters. Some are decidedly wacky (for example, some of the management practices of some Silicon Valley firms headed by religious people; but that is another story); some are significant indicators of a sea change. In March 2000, the Council of the Anglican Provinces of Africa held a conference with World Bank officials entitled A*lleviating Poverty in Africa*. The final communiqué includes the words: 'We agree that the spiritual dimension of life is an essential component of development.'[1] Food for thought.

WHAT DO FAIR TRADERS SAY?

In April 1996 in the first week after Easter, ninety-seven Traidcraft Fair Traders (and others) journeyed to Iona. It was billed as a retreat, but they renamed it an advance. In *Justice & Peace Prayers,* the booklet that came out of that week,[2] you can read of how this 'Mary time for Marthas' joined the ideas of 'work as prayer' with 'prayer as work'. A key theme was that what we are is as important as what we do: "Now the being is going to come before the doing", as one participant expressed it.

Eva McNeill, Traidcraft's top selling Fair Trader, likes how this 'being' is captured in our logo.

It says to me that as an organisation we are vibrant, alive, on the move, reaching out to all peoples everywhere. And, most importantly, it's in the shape of a cross – it's Christian.

Eildon Dyer, who has been part of Traidcraft for many years, speaks of Traidcraft as part of a Christian struggle for justice:

> The good news that Jesus brought was about the kingdom, which isn't about airy fairy stuff in the hereafter. It's about bringing good news to the poor and giving them a fair reward for what they do. The church has a responsibility to act on that.[3]

Traidcraft's achievements in putting fair trade on the map for many people, outside the church as well as within it, is not in doubt. The Bishop of Guildford, the Rt Revd John Gladwin, says:

> Wherever I go I find Traidcraft stalls in churches and amongst Christian people. And people have become aware that when you purchase goods, it's not just a simple buying and selling relationship – there's a whole package of social issues that go with that. And I think Traidcraft's achieved a lot of that in the Christian community.[4]

A WAY FORWARD?

There are movements within Traidcraft that would diminish rather than build the Christian basis. In recent years the increasing professionalism of Traidcraft – which is both necessary and laudable – has led (perhaps inevitably?) to an emphasis on skills and abilities rather than organisational 'fit' in the selection of staff. This has led to a reduced 'buy in' to the Christian basis from some staff. And it is true that some segments of the market are alienated by the profile of Traidcraft as faith-based. So some aspects of sales and marketing have downplayed the Christian distinctive in recent years. The drive to increase Fair Trader numbers outside the church has been successful, but the sales values and likely 'life-time' of the 'new wave' may prove to be less substantial than that of their forebears. The way forward is not so much a dilution of the Christian basis as a reinterpretation of it.

At its core such a reinterpretation must include a spiritual view of the whole of life. Spiritual awareness could be described as that sense that 'there is more to life than meets the eye.' We should reject that atomisation that divides and separates us as individuals and instead welcome the necessary belonging of individuals in community (and of communities in their environment). This integrated vision means that the spiritual dimension that connects meaning and purpose to values and so to actions is a part of the whole of the cosmos. This way of seeing things is the antithesis of the privatisation of faith. Rather it celebrates the network of connections joining the action (fair trading) with the values (supremely respect for the human person) and the meaning and purpose (of the world as created, redeemed and sustained by God, as seen in Jesus).

This reinterpretation acknowledges with gratitude those with whom we share actions and values, but not faith – but also sees limitations to secular humanism as a full and complete response to the world. From a Christian perspective it is plain that for people of goodwill to do their best is just not enough as a response to the manifold evils of the world. And so Traidcraft should embody a radical Christian spirituality. The 'marks' of that distinctively Christian spirituality could be many. Some of the key distinctives are:

- *Hope* – Christian faith is one of hope, and not hope that we might somehow escape – but that God will redeem that which is. 'He [Jesus] will come again to judge the living and the dead', declares the Apostles' Creed – an ultimate hope for justice.
- *Incarnation* – 'God with us', in humility identifying with the losers in our world, is the mark of Christ's work and should mark Christian work.
- *The cross* – To succeed through failure may seem nonsense but, again, a Christian spirituality is to pray that 'we may find the way of the cross none other than the way of life and peace.'
- *The suffering servant* – Jesus modelled the self-giving which is the mark of Christian discipleship when he 'emptied himself, taking the form of a servant' (Philippians 2).

Much of the work of Traidcraft's Fair Traders does bear these marks. Choosing them for Traidcraft as a whole is a challenge to which we need to rise. A key part of that will be to celebrate and build what we *are*, as well as to do well what we do.

BEING A CHRISTIAN-BASED TRAIDCRAFT

Traidcraft has a mission: to 'fight poverty through trade'. And that mission is unpacked in terms of goals (to 'double impact by the year 2002' – from a 1998 baseline) and 'signs of success' ('improving the lives of "third world" producers', etc.). The values statement that was prepared in 1998 to accompany that mission and goals statement was:

> *Traidcraft is a Christian response to poverty. It strives to*
> * *Show a bias to the poor*
> * *Respect people and the environment*
> * *Be transparent and accountable*
> * *Show creativity and innovation*
> * *Be the best*

In recent years we have rightly made much of the mission statement: the values statement has not had the same emphasis. Fair traders are asking Traidcraft to give it more. The values statement can be a basis for a clear and consistent message about Traidcraft's Christian basis and as such should be part of the message on all communications materials of sufficient substance to include any message about what we are and do. (In the latter part of the '90s it would have been possible to be recruited as a Fair Trader and get deeply stuck in to Traidcraft without ever knowing of the Christian basis.) All events – perhaps especially Fair Trader events – should include programme elements that explicitly address the spiritual basis of Traidcraft. These events, and in particular the worship elements led by Wild Goose, from the Iona Community, have been formative for some Fair Traders. The sense of 'family' they engender is key to making sense of the Gateshead connection, which can otherwise seem remote, and to fostering solidarity. Fair Traders are seeking 'spiritual refreshment' to be part of their experience of Traidcraft.

Traidcraft's Christian basis is reflected in our partnerships. Traidcraft's longest and most loyal partners are Christian Aid, CAFOD and SCIAF. That our partnerships should be with the official aid agencies of the Protestant and Catholic Churches is entirely appropriate. That Traidcraft is sometimes seen as 'the trading arm of Christian Aid' may be incorrect – but is a back-handed compliment. And about a third of Fair Traders donate their 'profits' to Christian Aid or to CAFOD.

Traidcraft has recognised and responded to the church environment from which many representatives are drawn and in which many sell. The Love, Justice, Trade poster set ("A resource which explores the links between Christian beliefs and fair trade in action through reflections and poems, and traditional prayers from the 'third world'") is a case in point. But many Fair Traders struggle to find acceptance for the idea of Traidcraft in their churches and need more resources. Mass communications materials that make the case for Traidcraft as a normal part of Christian discipleship are especially important.

WILL IT WORK?

Will an increased emphasis on a reinterpreted Christian basis work, or will it marginalise Traidcraft and diminish its impact? These are central questions. Experiential evidence is that there is a correlation between top-selling Fair Traders and those who are Christian. (One 'key contact' [a 'super' Fair Trader who supports other Fair Traders] suggested that 90 per cent of active Fair Traders have church connections.) This could, of course, be a correlation with no causal link. (However, for many Fair Traders their sense of justice has deep roots in Christian faith – and the 'faith $\rightarrow$ sense of justice $\rightarrow$ activity as a Fair Trader' set of connections is important.) But market research, undertaken by Traidcraft in 1998, shows that in terms of motivation, Christian faith is the second most significant motivator for Fair Traders.

The 'third way' may be last year's slogan, but for Traidcraft it may be a term whose time has come. The 'new Traidcraft', if unfairly caricatured as 'sales at any price managed by sharp professionals whose ethics only just cover their personal ambition', is a future which is probably both unattainable and undesirable. The same could be said for the 'old Traidcraft', if unfairly characterised as 'their hearts in the right place, but they couldn't organise a party in a brewery.' Can a 'third way' hold together the radical Christian discipleship that gave depth and distinctiveness to Traidcraft (indeed which defines Traidcraft) with the professionalism needed to succeed? The answer may lie in what we mean by a Christian basis.

HOW CAN A CHRISTIAN BASIS BE INCLUSIVE?

The reinterpretation of the Christian basis of Traidcraft must be inclusive rather than exclusive. Traidcraft grew out of an earlier organisation which was perceived to be too exclusive, in particular with reference to those it purchased goods from. If Traidcraft is to be inclusive, then it may need to owe more to the process by which we make our pilgrimage (being on a journey and inviting all to join us) than to a dogma by which we stake our ground (by definition to the exclusion of others). In a postmodern world it may be that our creeds answer questions that no one is asking, and that what is needed is an approach that is lighter on analysis and words, and stronger on direction and empathy. Traidcraft has a basis of faith – a creed written twenty years ago. It is not part of the everyday tools of Fair Traders. The Gospels are not lists of putative objective truth, but they are full of stories … and prayers. The Lord's Prayer may be the pattern we seek. Following Tom Wright in *The Lord and His Prayer* (SPCK, London, 1996):

Our Father in heaven, hallowed be your name.
'Father' to Jesus' hearers spoke of God saving his people through the Exodus. The challenge to us personally to follow entails risk: for Jesus – the carpenter – it ended in wood and nails. But Christian spirituality is nothing less than 'the rhythm of standing in the presence of the pain of the world, and kneeling in the presence of the creator of the world; of bringing those things together in the name of Jesus.' (p. 22)

Your kingdom come, your will be done, on earth as it is in heaven.
'We can only pray this prayer if we are prepared to mean: make us Kingdom bearers!… Make us, in turn, Servants of the Lord.' (p. 32)

Give us today our daily bread.
'We offer ourselves, in this prayer, as representatives of the world (this is what it means to be a "royal priesthood") turning into words the unspoken prayer from thousands of hungry folk

in our own country and millions around the world.' (p. 46)

Forgive us our sins, as we forgive those who sin against us.
'To pray this prayer is therefore, in its largest meaning, to pray for the world ... lift up your eyes ... and see the world as a whole, groaning in travail, longing for peace and justice.' (p. 57).

See also the image of 'a young Jewish boy off in the far country feeding the pigs ... Allow your praying heart ... to see the Father doing the unthinkable, the disgraceful thing, and running down the road to meet his muddled and muddy son. As we pray this prayer for the world, let us be alert to new visions of what the living God wants us to aim at in our society. Could it be that we could work and pray for a Jubilee?' (p. 58)

Lead us not into temptation, but deliver us from evil.
That deliverance is costly. 'As Schweitzer once put it, Jesus was called to throw himself on the wheel of history so that, even though it crushed him, it might start to turn in the opposite direction.' (p. 69)

'You can't pray these prayers from a safe distance ... We are called to live and pray at the place where the world is in pain, so that the hopes and fears, the joy and pain of the whole world may become, by the Spirit and in our own experience, the joy and pain of God.' (pp. 75–76)

For the kingdom, the power, and the glory are yours, now and for ever. Amen.
'This is the prayer of mission and commission. If Jesus is the true King of all the world, whose kingdom redefines power and glory so that they are now seen in the manger, on the cross, and in the garden, then to pray this prayer is to pray that this kingdom, this power and this glory be seen in all the world. It is not enough, although it is the essential starting-point, that we submit in our own lives to God's alternative kingdom-vision; we must pray and work for the vision to become in reality, with the rulers of this world confronted with their rightful king.' (p. 86)

A BETTER WAY?

A Traidcraft whose life is shaped by such a Christian spirituality will be very different from an organisation aiming for similar outcomes but based purely on generally accepted best practice. It will certainly be the antithesis of a 'me too' organisation. Traidcraft's history is one of creativity and innovation.

Could it be that listening to the 'community's wisdom' in the collective memory of thousands of Fair Traders will keep Traidcraft developing its understanding of itself as a Christian organisation, and so keeping it in the place of real creativity?

THE LAST WORD

Iona Sermon

> Lord, help me to surrender
> My heart to your love,
> My will to your rule,
> My weakness to your power,
> My life to your purposes.
>
> Lord, help me to struggle
> Against the oppression of the poor,
> Against the tyranny of injustice,
> Against the evil of racism,
> Against the powers of darkness.
>
> Lord, help me to suffer
> In the hunger of the deprived,
> In the pain of the rejected,
> In the despair of the hopeless,
> In the broken-ness of the world.
>
> Lord, in surrender, struggle, suffering,
> I give myself totally to you:
> For I would not bring you an offering
> That costs me nothing.[5]

NOTES

1   'Christian Faith and Economics Revisited 2: A New Partnership for Poverty Alleviation in Africa', *Transformation* October 2000, Vol. 7 No. 4, p. 123. See also Belshaw et al., cited in Note 4, p. 89.

2   *Justice and Peace Prayers* (Traidcraft, Gateshead, 1996).

3   Personal communication.

4   Traidcraft 'Celebrity' video (1998).

5   *Justice and Peace Prayers*, p. 7.

Chapter Eight

Traidcraft's Christian Basis
and the Secular Market Place

An exploration of the issues surrounding
an understanding of working in markets

Stuart Raistrick

Traidcraft fights poverty through trade.

Traidcraft's original foundation principles referred to 'establishing a just trading system which expresses the principles of love and justice fundamental to the Christian faith.'[1] That system would be based on service and equity, aim to remedy gross material inequalities and make commercial decisions by reference to the life of Jesus and his example. The key part of this aim, which implicitly condemns the methods of trading presently in existence, is the establishment of a 'just trading system'.

Adopting such aims led to Traidcraft and other similar organisations that sprang up in most developed countries being labelled generically as 'alternative trading organisations' or ATOs. Today the international umbrella organisation of such ATOs (and the producers in poor countries with whom they deal) is the International Federation of Alternative Trade (IFAT). In one way or another, all the buyers in the developed world who are part of IFAT subscribe to the aim of establishing a distinctly different trading system and so subverting the market place.

Traidcraft, in common with some but not all ATOs, is a Christian based company. This chapter will review the history of the belief that a different trading system could be established;

explore alternative Christian ideas about markets; briefly review the importance of economic growth; and discuss the way in which ideas of community are vital to markets. Finally, it will conclude that Traidcraft and its supporters should abandon antipathy to free markets.

THE ROOTS OF CHRISTIAN SOCIAL ACTION
AND OF TRAIDCRAFT

Unrest with the established economic order has been a feature of the life of many Christians in the United Kingdom for about 150 years. In 1994, John Atherton was Canon Theologian at Manchester Cathedral, a lecturer in Theology at Manchester University and Secretary of the William Temple Society, when he wrote *Social Christianity – a Reader.*[2] This book is a useful survey of the way that Christian thought has developed on the questions that are being discussed in this chapter. Atherton identifies the moment when the problem of the exploitation of workers and the need to do something about it led to the beginnings of a movement for Christian socialism and a great debate about the way Christians ought to behave in relation to markets. The moment was 10 April 1848, when F. D. Maurice, Charles Kingsley and John Ludlow drew up the first of many tracts arguing against the 'conservative orthodoxies of the establishments of churches and society'[3] and in favour of 'a bold commitment to the growing army of urban and rural poor.'[4]

There is a parallel between the actions of these founders of Christian socialism and the founders of Traidcraft and other ATOs throughout the developed world. The early Christian socialists raised their voices in protest at some of the injustices of the industrial revolution and the social changes in England in the middle of the nineteenth century. The ATO movement is reacting against the injustices of globalisation and reflecting the increased awareness about world poverty that developed in the latter half of the twentieth century.

F. D. Maurice challenged his hearers in 1851 to consider that,

> … the gospel must be either thrown away by Englishmen altogether, as a tale of other days, or recognised as the law of all their public and private life, of their inner selves, of their outward

transactions.'[5]

Richard Adams, who founded Traidcraft, wrote in 1989,

> Christians too are coming to accept that no longer can they talk of salvation in purely spiritual, other-worldly terms....[6]
>
> Jesus gives us a personal mission statement which demands a total realignment of ourselves, a goal in which conventional achievement has no place, where material values are discarded and where service, not excellence, is the final criterion for judgement.[7]

Both writers are in the same tradition demanding a conversion to a view of personal and social action which is gospel based, which 'expresses the principles of love and justice fundamental to the Christian faith.'[8]

F. D. Maurice and Richard Adams both seem to be calling for a primarily moral crusade rather than founding a political or economic movement (although there may be political or economic consequences). The needs of the world economy must be tested against the moral demands of the gospel. The moral demands must prevail. Referring to 'excellence, achievement, enterprise and all the other qualities that are linked with work and business', Adams puts it, in his book *Who Profits?*, that 'they need to be set in their rightful place, which must be firmly anchored in a moral framework.'[9] The conclusion of Adams, like Maurice before him (and many others such as Westcott, Temple, Tawney, Newbiggin and best of all probably Moltmann), is that the moral demands of the Christian faith require that free markets be either moderated by some intervention or replaced by a completely different system to ensure justice and equality.

Richard Adams speculates that after poverty is defeated then 'the longer-term programme would need to be set in place: making a fundamental change in our global economy to give fair trading conditions to all and down-scaling the lifestyle of the rich 20 per cent to create a sustainable future for our planet.'[10]

Traidcraft is founded on this premise. The gospel demands social action to free poor people from their enslavement to poverty. This impulse has led to the creation of a successful ATO, a successful charity working to educate and empower poor people in trade and the involvement of thousands of producers and customers throughout the world. But the theology at the heart of Traidcraft is a theology in the mainstream of the English tradition of social Christianity. It believes in intervention and does not support the free operation of markets. Adams looks for 'a fundamental change' and Traidcraft's original Foundation Principles implicitly condemn the present market-based structure of world trade.

THE CHRISTIAN COMMITMENT TO A FREE MARKET

Although the majority of Christian writers on economic matters during the twentieth century have tended to a Christian socialist view there have been exceptions. In the latter part of the eighteenth century and the early years of the nineteenth writers were setting out a theological basis for believing that free markets were best. According to this stream of Christian thought, markets are held to work for three reasons. They provide the right incentives for people in that initiative, industriousness and creativity are rewarded, incentives that God built into His creation. They enable choices to be made and the subsequent allocation of resources to be carried out in the most efficient way despite the sinful nature of the people making the choices. But there is a deeper reason why markets work. They allow for an infinite number of types of human and human views of the world in line with the way God created us all. We are not all the same, nor even all Christian, but markets let us freely work together to promote economic growth.

Writers from the eighteenth and nineteenth century such as T. R. Malthus and J. B. Sumner have been joined in the latter part of the twentieth century by others, notably Brian Griffiths from the UK and Michael Novak from the USA.

These writers argue that the competitiveness of markets is part of creation. God made us free and different from each other. So Novak wrote in 1982,

> A democratic capitalist society mirrors the infinity of God through the conflicting discordant, irreconcilable differences of

huge numbers of persons, each of whom is an originating agency of distinctive insight and distinctive choice.[11]

Markets help us provide free choices to each other and establish an arena free from coercion in which we can all develop. Modern writers in this 'Christian conservative' tradition (I adopt this nomenclature following the example of John Atherton) have also been fervent in their support of democracy and have taken a very strong line on the importance of institutions in society being the means by which a moral framework is created and nurtured. The issue of the context for markets will be considered briefly later. Markets achieve one more remarkable thing. They assist economic growth. Speaking of market forces in 1996 in their publication *The Common Good*, the UK's Catholic Bishops said,

> No system has so far shown itself superior in encouraging wealth creation and hence in advancing the prosperity of the community, and enabling poverty and hardship to be more generously relieved.[12]

The accepted Christian orthodoxy that 'Any serious Christian must be a Socialist', as Paul Tillich is reported to have answered a student's query in 1957,[13] is beginning to be challenged. Christians who are concerned to fight poverty need to consider the theological arguments presented by writers in defence of markets. Arguments about creativity, freedom and just reward following initiative need to be grappled with because for many years the Christian conservative argument has been muted in the UK.

IS ECONOMIC GROWTH ANY GOOD?

Defenders of free markets usually end up, as the UK's Catholic Bishops did, by justifying markets in the following way: economic growth is promoted more effectively by markets than by any other system. Christian socialists tend to be prepared to accept restrictions in growth and less efficient markets provided certain moral criteria are met. Does this mean that markets are immoral in that there is less stress on the ethics and more on economic growth among their supporters? What is the importance of economic growth? For Traidcraft, dedicated to fighting poverty through trade, it is important to stand on firm ground to understand the importance of trade and economic growth.

The United Nations has published, each year since 1990, a report on the progress in Human Development of each member state. The Report also contains a league table of important indicators. In the very first report in 1990 the authors made the point that,

> In the long run, economic growth is crucial for determining whether countries can sustain progress in human development...[15]

We must not equate human development with economic growth: again to quote from the UN Report in 1990,

> The purpose of development is to offer people more options. One of their options is access to more income – not as an end in itself but as a means to acquiring human well-being. But there are other options as well, including long life, knowledge, political freedom, personal security, community participation and guaranteed human rights.[16]

However, we cannot ignore the statement that economic growth is crucial. 'Growth in the world's wealth is a compelling moral imperative if all are to be fed, clothed, housed and given the opportunity for self-realisation',[17] is how Novak expressed one of the strongest arguments for free markets.

THE KNOWLEDGE ARGUMENT FOR MARKETS

There are strong arguments for supporting markets. The main ones are well discussed in a great deal of literature but are sometimes called the 'epistemological' argument and the 'incentive' argument.

The first, the 'epistemological', is about knowledge. Because no-one can know the extent of all the resources that are available nor envisage the uses to which these resources might be put, it is argued that the role of the market is to make use of the scarcest resource of all – human knowledge. This is the way the argument was put by John Gray, the distinguished philosopher from Oxford in 1992.[18] This argument explains why command economies collapse and, in the right political conditions, market economies succeed. It is impossible for those who would intervene or control a market to have sufficient information.

THE INCENTIVE ARGUMENT FOR MARKETS.

The second, the 'incentive', draws on the way that perverse, unhelpful incentives are created by economies that are not free, preferring low risk and rewarding safe mediocrity rather than flair. Meanwhile market economies reward initiative and efficiency and create incentives that support growth.

Both these arguments have their theological supporters and detractors. Christians might not be convinced merely by argument but want to know how the arguments fit with their understanding of how God would prefer things to be. My view is that these philosophical arguments support the Christian conservative stance. The epistemological argument fits with the way God created us all to be free and the incentive argument deals with the need to constrain our sinful tendencies.

One other debate about markets needs to be aired. This is the question of the context in which they exist. It has been common ground since Aristotle, I believe, that wealth is not an end but merely a means to an end. 'Wealth is evidently not the good we are seeking, for it is merely useful and for the sake of something else',[19] is the quote from Aristotle used approvingly by the authors of the UN Report referred to earlier. At Traidcraft, wealth created through trade is the means by which we hope to see poverty relieved. The wealth itself is the means to this end. But we want more. Relieving poverty but leaving people in a moral and spiritual vacuum would not be an acceptable outcome. Poverty of spiritual life through false belief or no belief at all is just as serious. Christian conservatives have tended to argue that markets only make sense as part of a necessary panoply of free democratic institutions. The requirements for economic growth are held (by Novak and others) to be a democratic polity, social institutions which create and defend an ethical framework and a free market.

MARKETS DEPEND ON COMMUNITY

This, I think, leads to a further insight. Markets depend on community. Wherever markets operate successfully they are based in some sort of community, whether it be the small local village or a nation state or worldwide. In Hexham, the rural town where I am writing this piece, a market has operated by Royal charter since the thirteenth century. From the earliest days, the traders in the market have developed rules to ensure fair trading, to settle weights and measures disputes and problems of stolen goods. The market developed within its community. It is impossible to envisage a market working at all without contact between its members, a degree of trust and mutual interest and a high level of communication. Those of us who have, at times, had to sell goods and services know that human contact is what creates the sale. It is not just a matter of price and availability. Even the new dot.com traders know this. They are all working hard to create communities of people attracted to their sites not just by the goods and services on offer but by other intangible benefits such as discussion and interaction to create that community that the market needs if it is to flourish. So, in a very real sense, the operation of markets contributes to the creation of community. Often trade is the very first link between groups of people. Following trade other connections are made. Fighting poverty through trade is more than just increasing wealth, although that is vital. It is about creating the first stages of community. Partly this is why the birth pangs of the global economy are so painful. The sense of a global community is developing at the same time and is a prerequisite if trade is to be successfully conducted. But new communities require new relationships; maybe even the breaking off of some old relationships, and this is hurtful. Meanwhile, in the absence of a community, the global market is less constrained by the democratic and social institutions that are needed as its context. This results in behaviour by some confirming that sinfulness abounds. It is to be hoped that the global market does its part in creating a global sense of community sooner rather than later.

IMPLICATIONS FOR TRAIDCRAFT

Traidcraft's original Foundation Principles referred to 'establishing a just trading system which expresses the principles of love and justice fundamental to the Christian faith.' The features of that system were to be that it would be based on service and equity, aim to remedy gross material inequalities and make commercial decisions by reference to the life of Jesus and his example.

The main change in the last twenty-one years has been the realisation that the trading system that is likely to have these features is one that is based on the free market. Revised Foundation Principles, developed in 1999 (see Appendix Two), omit the reference to establishing a just trading system and instead begin by stating

Traidcraft is a Christian response to poverty

Enforced poverty is a gross affront to both the goodness of God as creator in providing for all his creatures and the well-being of human beings.

An appropriate Christian response will be marked by:
- A partnership between rich and poor;
- Positively affirming the call to all people to steward and develop the creation;
- Service, equity and justice, which address both persons and processes in wider society; and
- A bias to the poor.

Only in recent years have theologians set out the reasons why free markets produce better results. This chapter has tried to point out some of the writers to whom readers can refer to review these arguments for themselves.

Traidcraft operates in many markets. It buys goods, craft products and food, worldwide. It sells, in competition with many other retailers, to UK consumers. We provide services for producers such as product development help, market access advice and so on. To advance the autonomy of producers these services are not 'handed out' but are the subject of contracts. Traidcraft has established (and continues establishing) partner organisations in the developing world. So that autonomy can flourish these partners are independent and make their own decisions. We sell to them and compete to provide the best services we can to them. Traidcraft operates in the market for staff. The skills and experience needed are scarce and recruiting and retaining them is difficult.

We must see ourselves not as overthrowing the market system but working within it. That is not to say that our behaviour should be any less moral or just but that we recognise the need to work within the world as it is. We need to recognise that markets are an inevitable result of having to grapple with the sinfulness that has arisen out of the personal freedom God created for us. If so we should accept this and get on with working within the market to achieve the best for our customers and producers. We should not pretend, especially to the poor in the Two-Thirds World,[20] that we know a better answer.

We must accept the limitations of markets. Other peoples' choices affect the range of goods and services that can be traded so that there is no subjective test or prediction of what will work or what will fail. The whole process is one of trial and error, hopefully with increasing skill. The only guaranteed outcome is failure if we withdraw from the market altogether. Therefore, if we are to help others to trade and trade ourselves, part of our job is to increase understanding of the way markets work and help people develop the skills needed to succeed. For this reason the work carried on by Traidcraft, to work with and build capacity in two-thirds world producers, is especially important if the fight against poverty is to be successful.

A key signal in markets is price. Where we operate we must recognise that the market price is the price at which we need to buy and sell. This applies equally in the market from which we recruit staff. If we need a premium price for goods they must have a premium quality. The premium quality we most often offer is 'fair trade'. This reputation must be guarded and enhanced. If we need to buy goods at a price that is higher than the market price because in our judgement to do so would be just (and this often happens) then recouping that price through fair trade depends on Traidcraft being recognised as a leader in just trading practices. Nothing that diminishes that reputation can be allowed to occur.

If it is accepted that markets work best in communities then Traidcraft has a role to develop the communities in which it operates. This ensures that trade takes place within a helpful context. Our campaign, during 1999 and 2000, to introduce an element of social reporting into the revised company legislation in the UK is an example of this in practice. If UK companies, many of which trade with the developing world, have to report on their social conduct and its effect, there will be pressure to trade fairly applied to large companies by public and share-holder opinion. A change in UK law might have a multiplied effect across the globe if it is seen to be effective by campaign-ers in other countries. So a few thousands of pounds invested in a campaign in an arcane area of UK company law might do more to relieve poverty than any number of fair trade transac-tions through catalogue sales. Working to create and influence the community (in the widest sense) institutions that create the context for markets is a vital field of activity.

CONCLUSION

The years roll on and theological ideas change too. Our under-standing is changed as circumstances change, as we develop and as the Holy Spirit inspires us. I believe that ideas about mar-kets in Christian theology and especially in the community at Traidcraft are changing too.

Free markets promote economic growth for very good rea-sons. They are in tune with God's creation and are part of creat-ing as Novak wrote in 1982 'a noncoercive society as an arena of liberty, within which individuals and peoples are called to realise, through democratic methods, the vocations to which they believe they are called.'[21]

Markets are not an evil influence enslaving people but rather a mechanism to promote economic growth and individual freedom.

BIBLIOGRAPHY

Adams, Richard, *Who Profits?* (Oxford: Lion Publishing, 1989).
Atherton, John, *Social Christianity – a reader* (London: SPCK, 1994).

Catholic Bishops' Conference of England and Wales, *The Common Good and the Catholic Church's Social Teaching* (Manchester: Gabriel Communications, 1996).

Gray, John, *The Moral Foundations of Market Institutions* (London: IEA Health and Welfare Unit, 1992).

Griffiths, Brian, *Morality and the Market Place: Christian alternatives to Capitalism and Socialism* (London: Hodder and Stoughton, 1982).

Griffiths, Brian, *The Creation of Wealth* (London: Hodder and Stoughton, 1984).

Hayek, Frederich A., *The Road to Serfdom* (University of Chicago Press 1994, first published in 1944).

Malthus, T. R., *An essay on the principle of population as it affects the future improvement of society* (London: Penguin Books, 1970; first published London: Johnson, 1798).

Moltmann, Jürgen, *The Trinity and the Kingdom of God* (Minneapolis: Augsberg Fortress Publishers, 1993).

Newbiggin, Lesslie, *Foolishness to the Greeks: The Gospel and Western Culture* (London: SPCK, 1986).

Novak, Michael, *The Spirit of Democratic Capitalism* (London: IEA Health and Welfare Unit, 1991).

Temple, William, *Christianity and Social Order* (London: SPCK, 1976; first published London: Penguin Books, 1942).

United Nations Human Development Report 1990 (Oxford: Oxford University Press, 1990 and each year since).

Valelly, Paul, *The New Politics: Catholic Social Teaching for the Twenty-First Century* (London: SCM Press, 1998).

Weber, Max, *The Theory of Social and Economic Organisation* (New York: The Free Press, 1964; first published New York: Oxford University Press, 1947).

Weber, Max, *The Protestant Ethic and the Spirit of Capitalism* (London and New York: Routledge, 1992; first published New York: HarperCollins Academic, 1930). Novak deliberately echoes the title of this seminal work in *The Spirit of Democratic Capitalism*: see above.

NOTES

1   *Deed of mutual covenant* 19 July 1986, Second Schedule, Clause 1.

2   John Atherton, *Social Christianity – a reader* (London: SPCK, 1994).

3   Atherton, *Social Christianity*, p. 13.

4   Atherton, *Social Christianity*, p. 13.

5   Frederick D. Maurice, *Reasons for Co-operation*, a lecture delivered at the Office for Promoting Working Men's Associations on 11 December 1850, quoted by Atherton, *Social Christianity*, p. 77.

6   Richard Adams, *Who Profits?* (Oxford: Lion Publishing, 1989), p. 49.

7   Adams, *Who Profits?*, p. 50.

8   *Deed of mutual covenant* 19 July 1986, Second Schedule, Clause 1.

9   Adams, *Who Profits?*, p. 46.

10   Adams, *Who Profits?*, p. 49.

11   Michael Novak, *The Spirit of Democratic Capitalism* (London: IEA Health and Welfare Unit, 1991; first published Maryland, USA: Madison Books, 1982), p. 64.

12   Catholic Bishops' Conference of England and Wales, *The Common Good and the Catholic Church's Social Teaching* (Manchester: Gabriel Communications, 1996), para. 78.

13   This exchange is reported in J. Philip Wogaman, *The Great Economic Debate* (Philadelphia: Westminster Press, 1977), p. 133.

15   *United Nations Human Development Report 1990* (Oxford: Oxford University Press, 1990), p. 3.

16   *United Nations Human Development Report 1990* (Oxford: Oxford University Press, 1990), p. iii.

17   Novak, *Spirit of Democratic Capitalism*, p. 264.

18   John Gray, *The Moral Foundation of Market Institutions* (London: IEA Health and Welfare Unit, 1992), pp. 5–17, for a full discussion of the epistemological and incentive arguments.

19   *United Nations Human Development Report 1990*, p. 9.

20   The preferred self-definition of those who live in situations of poverty and oppression, which affect two-thirds of the world's population, found both in highly developed and less developed countries.

21   Novak, *Spirit of Democratic Capitalism*, p. 360.

Chapter Nine

Traidcraft and the Churches

Margaret Masson

INTRODUCTION

Traidcraft was started by a group of practical visionaries, Christians who believed that central to the Christian vocation is the call to justice and to make a tangible difference in this world. They were pioneers and purists; the way they pursued justice was just as important to them as the results achieved. Traidcraft's first supporters were church people. Twenty-one years on, its largest group of supporters is still mainly drawn from the churches.

Yet, in its twenty-one year history, Traidcraft has grown significantly, changed inevitably. The sympathies of its supporter base and its staff is wider than at its inception: many who would not identify themselves as Christians, but who share with Christians a passion for justice, work for Traidcraft as employees, fair traders and donors. And Traidcraft's sphere of influence in our culture is most telling today beyond the walls of the churches: in the market place, on government policy and in the growing awareness of the issues surrounding fair trade in British society as a whole.

With growth and coming of age come the inevitable questions of identity. One strand of such probing of identity is Traidcraft's continuing relationship with the churches. Has this kept pace with what Traidcraft has grown into? Can a synergy be assumed in the way it may have been in the early years? Has Traidcraft spent enough time and energy in recent years thinking through its present relationship with the churches and how it wishes to shape this more purposively? The answer to all these questions is: probably not. Traidcraft has tended to take for granted its relationship with the churches over the years. It has counted on their good will whilst rightly concentrating its energies on the business of trying to alleviate poverty in the Third World through fair trade. Traidcraft has looked to the churches for support, and especially for a continuing stream of fair traders, who are the very backbone of the business. It has assumed that the church stands behind it while Traidcraft itself looks out and beyond the church to the world it seeks to help transform. And in many ways, this outward-looking stance is very attractive. It has been this practical antidote to hand-wringing despair, this refreshing can-do attitude that has made Traidcraft, in relation to its size, remarkably successful and often inspirational. At twenty-one, there is much to congratulate and celebrate in Traidcraft. But significant birthdays are times for reflection as well as celebration, for introspection as well as for hopeful anticipation. It is in this spirit that this chapter considers the question of Traidcraft's relationship with the churches at this juncture in its history.

A PROPHETIC WITNESS

In its early years, Traidcraft served as a prophetic witness to the churches. It was small and little known, but for those Christians who did come into contact with it, Traidcraft offered a practical way of contributing to an important strand of what the gospel is all about, and possibly even helped them to reimagine what it means to be the church. The church is the people of God in a place coming together to worship, to bear witness to the Kingdom of God in a community. This theme of the Kingdom of God is a recurring one in the Bible: God's people gathered, God's Kingdom coming, God's reign inaugurated. This was what was yearned for, dreamed about by the prophets, and rejoiced in by the Gospel writers. And it was often imagined in terms of a restored justice, an overflowing sense of abundant life for all. This was the vision, the dream, which was both gift and goal. We see it in Isaiah, a prophet anointed by the Lord 'to bring good news to the oppressed, to bind up the broken hearted, to proclaim liberty to the captives, and release to the prisoners.' In

Luke's Gospel, these are the words that Jesus reads when he inaugurates his public ministry in the synagogue and it is these sentiments again which are echoed by Mary in the Magnificat: 'He has brought down the powerful from their thrones, and lifted up the lowly, he has filled the hungry with good things, and sent the rich away empty' (Lk. 1: 52–53). This vision of justice, of plenitude for all, is right at the heart of how God's Kingdom is imagined throughout the Bible.

INVITATION TO A FEAST

A whole plethora of images are used to invoke this vivid sense of God's Kingdom. My favourite is the image of the feast, the great banquet to which all are invited, with a particular emphasis on those usually excluded: the poor, the sick, the lame. This image of the feast is the basis for the symbolism of the communion service, central to worship in most Christian denominations. And part of its power is the way in which it takes what is essential to human life – food and eating and community – and helps us to see that this very ordinary, necessary, human activity is imbued with spiritual significance. As an image, the feast is practical and down-to-earth as well as celebratory; it helps to root our spirituality in the here and now of our material physicality even whilst we look forward to the beauty of heaven. Throughout the Bible, this image and this theme recurs again and again. Central to what it means to be God's people, God's church, is this call to hospitality, this invitation to include in very practical, physical ways, the poor, the disadvantaged, those on the margins. Comfortable complacency is repeatedly castigated. We cannot please God if we ignore our neighbour who is suffering great need whilst we have much more than we could ever use. If we do not care about such things, then we are far from the heart of the God who does care passionately and must at least question our right to call ourselves his faithful people.

Yet all too often in our churches, such a commitment to the poor is seen as an optional extra for those who are especially keen or trendy or 'into that kind of thing'. Sometimes it is dismissed as mere 'social gospel' or, heaven forbid, 'mixing politics with religion'. A commitment to the poor and to seeking the justice of God's Kingdom is not, by and large in British churches today, assumed to be central to the identity of the church, to being a Christian. Such a climate means that the message of Traidcraft is by no means a given in our churches. How often do we hear sermons which talk about fair trade, or which challenge us, as a members of the church, about our responsibility to do something about the injustices in our world? We do not forget, of course, that it is thanks to the support of many church people that Traidcraft survives. Yet if the support of these few – support not necessarily for Traidcraft, as such, but for the commitments to the disadvantaged of our world it espouses – were considered the norm for church members rather than a minority interest, how much more could be done to alleviate poverty? How much more potently could the church then witness to the coming of God's Kingdom?

This care for the poorest of the poor, this sense of responsibility to work for justice, is at the heart of what Traidcraft is about. It should also be at the heart of what the church is about – both the church as an institution and each and every gathering of Christians. Church is not a club, it is not a form of entertainment or place to meet those who share our values and make friends. It should be a place of radical hospitality that witnesses to the kind of banquet that Jesus himself hosts.

NETWORKING FOR JUSTICE

So my key question for Traidcraft in the year of its coming of age is, are we doing enough of this prophetic witness within the churches? I want to argue that Traidcraft should be more self consciously facing two ways, not just serving as salt and light in the market place of the secular world, vital as that continues to be, but also challenging and seeking to transform the church which lies behind it. Perhaps part of Traidcraft's job is to help to remind the church that working towards justice, helping the poor, is a central part of our calling, part of what it means to be disciples of Christ. In recent years, Traidcraft has done excellent advocacy work in the political arena. Within the organisation, there is anticipation as well as satisfaction about the work of the relatively new policy unit's work as it tries to help shape business and commercial culture, both in the UK and overseas. But what are we doing to influence the thinking of those in our churches? There is no current strategy for this, no real sense at present that this is a priority, possibly even an important part of Traidcraft's mission.

If Traidcraft were to consider putting more energy into its relationship with the churches, how might this kind of influence best be achieved? Such influence will never be the core aim of the organisation – its core aim must continue to be the alleviation of poverty through trade – so maximum effect for minimum energy is crucial. The obvious way of trying to achieve greater influence with greatest efficiency is networking. Traidcraft has shown itself to be an extremely effective networker in a number of spheres – social accounting, the corporate governance debate, the Ethical Trading Initiative, to name the obvious examples – sometimes having a surprising degree of influence in relation to its size. We need to identify some of the strategic people within particular branches of the church, people with influence, authority, those to whom significant numbers of people will listen. No doubt there are those among such leaders who would already be very sympathetic to what Traidcraft stands for. Some might be approached to be patrons, sponsors of Traidcraft. Traidcraft would need to think carefully about how best such people could be informed and inspired about Traidcraft's vision and work, and how they could be encouraged to actively look for opportunities to promote the Christian fair trade message. Traidcraft has neither the resources of time nor expertise to develop a comprehensive teaching programme for the churches. But if we could enlist, encourage, inspire some of the church's key teachers and leaders whose vocation is teaching and influencing the churches, then such networking could be potentially extremely fruitful.

It might also be worth trying to target the theological colleges of our land. Perhaps Traidcraft could aim to speak to each generation of potential Christian ministers and to ask them to consider how they might incorporate a fair trade message as part of their teaching and programmes of discipleship. Are we in touch with those who teach these ministers? They might also be encouraged to see if there is at least a little space on the (admittedly already overcrowded) curriculum for the challenge of this dimension of the gospel.

Traidcraft needs to inspire each generation of Christians afresh. It is probably fair to say that most of its most active supporters are no longer young. Is Traidcraft too exclusively rooted within the concerns of a particular Christian generation? Has it done enough to pass on the torch? If we do not bring the challenge to each new Christian generation, then Traidcraft will eventually wither, its vision perish. So, where are the points of church growth in our culture? Where are new churches flourishing, where are the young people flocking, who are their spiritual mentors and what kind of Christian values are they being taught? Is the fair trade message proclaimed at Spring Harvest, at Greenbelt, at Soul Survivor, in the Christian Unions and Scripture Unions of our land? We need more than stalls if we are serious about wanting to win people's minds and hearts as well as their money. Our aim should be to persuade them that fair trade is a radical, exciting, ethically-persuasive idea, not just a hobby for the keen few, or a commitment for those willing to be Fair Traders. Promoting and engaging in fair trade is one powerful way of being part of and witnessing to God's feast, to be considered, at least, as part of serious discipleship. Is it possible to suggest the fair trade message and activities as a part of Alpha and Emmaus discipleship courses? Fairly traded coffee and tea and wine and chocolate could add another rich dimension to the already inspired idea of evangelism and discipleship taking place in the context of a meal. Again, the image of the feast: it is not merely that food and drink create a pleasant ambience for introducing people to the faith: there is something profoundly theologically appropriate about such a context.

Of course Traidcraft could also try to make contact with some of the more formal church structures – the Boards of Social Responsibility and the like. But my sense is that those who are involved in such structures are probably already very sympathetic to ideas like fair trade. Their problem, like ours, is how to inspire others to consider and act on such commitments.

HOW IS TRAIDCRAFT SEEN BY THE CHURCHES?

If this chapter's first and main challenge to Traidcraft in its anniversary year is about reviving its prophetic role within the churches, the second question is closely related. How is Traidcraft seen by the churches? It would be useful for Traidcraft to know if church people have kept pace with how Traidcraft has changed and grown over the last two decades. And indeed, to what extent members are even aware of its existence. Sometimes, I am surprised at how little even well-informed people in the churches know about Traidcraft. 'Is that the same as Tearcraft?' can be one of the more enlightened responses. And for those who do know roughly what Traidcraft is about, are they still stuck with the image of 'buying a raffia basket to help the Third World'? Are they aware of the extent to which Traidcraft ought to be seen as part of a spearheading movement which aspires to inaugurate a new economic order, including ethical investment, an ethical view of the company, new forms of economic organisation? Traidcraft needs to think about how it communicates this vision of itself to the churches. It might be worth trying to find out what its profile and image actually is, and then considering a 'makeover' as it tries to bring the churches up-to-date with what Traidcraft is and what it is doing now it is twenty-one.

Investing this kind of energy on the churches takes time, imagination and resources. And all in a climate where all three are in great demand. But I do wonder if it is worth, even if just for a couple of years, investing in this kind of education and networking in a serious way.

HOW MIGHT THE CHURCHES SUPPORT TRAIDCRAFT?

So far, I have looked at what Traidcraft might be, perhaps ought to be, giving to the churches. But it is still important to ask how the churches might more effectively support the identity and work of Traidcraft. Without forgetting for a moment that thousands of faithful Christians throughout the country are the backbone of Traidcraft's activities, I believe that there is a great deal more Traidcraft might do to harness support and energy from the churches. Whilst Traidcraft is very aware of the work of Fair Traders and works hard to recruit and maintain them, it may not look hard enough at the other kinds of support from the wide range of people who might be sitting in the pews. Churchgoers include not only those willing to sell and buy fairly traded goods, but also teachers and politicians and business people, captains of industry, supermarket buyers, novelists, advertising executives, academics, journalists, indeed a whole range of the influential people who help to shape our culture and its values. Perhaps more of these people could be mobilised more effectively to challenge and influence the structures of which they are a part? Could they be more proactively encouraged to be part of a movement that gradually, but effectively is changing our culture? When I see the way in which fair trade has become so much more a part of mainstream thinking in the last few years, when I see supermarkets responding to what they perceive to be consumer demand for such products, I am greatly encouraged. How much more might be possible!

Traidcraft should also, I believe, expect to look to the churches to be funded, to be fed, theologically. I have been impressed by the way in which a number of Traidcraft staff do think theologically about what they are doing, and this despite the pressure of keeping a business going, or, in the case of Traidcraft Exchange, of running a rapidly growing charity. But again, Traidcraft may need to try to be a bit more proactive in asking for and harnessing some of the theological resources of our churches and academic institutions. Its leaders and staff may need to be encouraged to take time to be in touch with the kind of thinking that is shaping the market place, the way business is done, debates about new world orders, theological responses to global capitalism and so on. They need to be resourced to be engaged with and nourished by the kind of theology that might continue to give inspiration and encouragement as well as criticism and even guidance in the fair trade project. Vision cannot remain static or it will quickly ossify and die. And without vision, institutions as well as people perish.

Theologian Walter Brueggeman, in his book, *The Prophetic Imagination* (Philadelphia: Fortress Press, 1978) p. 13 argues that part of the job of the church is to fund an alternative imagination, the courage to think that it can be different. Too often, we feel despair in the face of all that is wrong in the world; the Two-Thirds World's suffering threatens to paralyse us by its overwhelming dimensions. We feel defeated by systems that seem beyond the power of humanity to change. Yet an alternative, Christian, prophetic imagination refuses to bow to the apparent inevitabilities of these injustices and sufferings. Instead, it seeks to offer glimpses of how God's way makes possible something very different. And Traidcraft is, for many, one such way. Traidcraft needs to draw on deep, prophetic thinking that will continue to renew the springs of its motivation and practice and energy; Traidcraft has much to contribute to such thinking in the way in which it is at the forefront of so much that is transformative. How can this symbiotic relationship between practice and reflection be encouraged and promoted? The promise of one small beginning is a Traidcraft Fellowship which has been set up in St Chad's College in Durham University.[1] This is an imaginative and encouraging move. But it must not serve as a kind of tokenism that allows anyone to think that Traidcraft's responsibility for deeper reflection is now met. The resources of the wider church are still of vital importance.

TRAIDCRAFT AND THE CHURCH OVERSEAS

One final set of questions that we might consider in trying to think through the relationship between Traidcraft and the churches cluster around the relationship between Traidcraft and the church overseas. Traidcraft's practice has been to work with partners, irrespective of their faith. In fact, this was one of the commitments that led to its separation from Tearcraft twenty-one years ago. It believed its mission was to work with the poorest of the poor, without making Christian adherence a precondition of partnership. Perhaps because of this, Traidcraft has never (to the best of my knowledge) had a strategy or policy about engagement with the church in a particular location. Because some of its partners are Christian, there are no doubt some informal links with local churches in some places. And in some countries where Christians are very much a minority, no doubt such links are virtually non-existent. One question that

Traidcraft might ask itself is this: in areas like South East Africa, where Traidcraft Exchange is expanding so rapidly – new partners now in Zambia, Malawi and Kenya to join those in South Africa and Tanzania – should Traidcraft be more actively trying to be make links with the churches in those countries? Very often such churches are also very much involved in working to alleviate poverty and to change structures which mitigate against justice. They are also often already extremely effective networks, influencing a much greater proportion of the population than is the case in the North.

No doubt there are sensitivities around this, and no doubt Traidcraft is acutely aware of these. But if it is to be more than just another kind of development agency, if it is to work out what it means to be a Christian organisation (and, of course, there have always been debates about what precisely it means for Traidcraft to be Christian) working to alleviate poverty through fair trade, then surely the question of how it engages with the mission of the local churches in the South cannot be ignored. More purposive links would allow the theology of the South increasingly to play a formative part in how Traidcraft works out its mission. The North's assumptions about wealth and development could be helpfully scrutinised by developing world perspectives and Traidcraft's impact would be more likely to be protected from the kind of distortions that must inevitably result from unmediated packages of assumptions about justice and development. And this kind of scrutiny could be fed back to the North, no doubt to the benefit of northern Christians struggling to discern God's prophetic imagination.

A FEAST FOR ALL

Yet again, when I think about the kind of relationships between Traidcraft and the churches I would like to see explored – churches of both North and South – the image that comes to mind is that of the feast. Gathered round a table laden with possibility, the relationships are inevitably reciprocal. The giving is mutual: one cannot feed without being fed oneself, the conversation is not a monologue, but a rich polyphony of voices. We taste the food, we savour the wine, we are brought alive by the stimulating diversity of the companionship. It is a foretaste of that heavenly banquet, the promise of the beauty of heaven where there is plenty for everyone – because God himself is the host.

NOTES

1   The Traidcraft Research Fellowship was set up in the Spring of 2000 as a joint venture between the Traidcraft Foundation and St Chad's College in the University of Durham. The purpose of the Fellowship is to help Traidcraft and other similar organisations to carry out their work more effectively, and in particular, to provide a more coherent theological framwork for their activities. The Fellow will also promote the discussion of fair trade issues in the College and the wider university. St Chad's College has a strong theological tradition. This tradition, combined with its current research into ethics and related areas, makes it an ideal location for the Fellowship. The first Fellow is now in post.

Chapter Ten

Resurrection and Hope: Traidcraft's Future

David Nussbaum

INTRODUCTION

The 'Hell Fire Club' had its home in the West Wycombe caves over two hundred years ago. If you visit the caves today, you walk a quarter of a mile along the tunnel into the hillside. There you can see displayed the text of a letter dated 3 May 1774 from one member of the club, Francis Dashwood, also known as Lord Le Despencer, to Benjamin Franklin. The two had collaborated over the construction of a more fuel-efficient stove and had engaged the services of a Mr Jackson to do so. Here is an extract from the letter, referring to this Mr Jackson:

> If you should meet this *fair trader* perhaps you will give yourself the trouble to speak to him at least to satisfy your curiosity and so that I may at least deal fairly by you.

So *fair trading* goes back a long way. Indeed, some of the parables of Jesus deal with the ethics of commercial enterprise, and he himself intervened to overturn unfair trading activities in the entrance area of the Temple in Jerusalem.

Traidcraft has been promoting fair trade for a rather shorter time. Looking ahead, what might its future include? What hopes might we hold for the future of this unusual, indeed unique organisation?

TRAIDCRAFT'S PURPOSE:
A CHRISTIAN RESPONSE TO POVERTY

The poor, Jesus told us, we would continue to have with us. So we can expect the need for a Christian response to poverty to remain - until Jesus returns and God makes all things new. So Traidcraft operates in this in-between time, when there is good news for the poor – but the poor are still with us and in need of this good news.

This eschatological combination of *already* (the stew is getting saltier) but *not yet* (only in places) is characteristic of our endeavours in Traidcraft, and we should expect it to continue like that, though with new and different manifestations. So *already* Traidcraft has built up a wealth of experience in promoting, supporting and engaging in fair trade, with a strong base of fair traders and donors, but it has *not yet* achieved sustained profitability (in the trading plc) sufficient to pay a dividend, or an appropriate level of reserves (in the charitable Exchange), for example.

What other *not yets* are there which Traidcraft may be able to address in the years ahead? One critical arena where change is needed is in the general appreciation of what 'fair trade' means. The Office of Fair Trading publishes its magazine *Fairtrading* quarterly, but its vision of what 'fair trading' means is restricted, focusing on 'anyone with an interest in consumer protection or competition policy.' Traidcraft's understanding of the world is that it is not just consumers but often also producers, especially primary producers and those who work in the production process, who need protection. Competition policy can be effective in protecting disparate consumers from powerful producers, but true fair trading also means protecting weaker producers and workers from markets that can operate to oppress them.

Traidcraft's pioneering work in social accounting and reporting has taken forward the debate about the relationships between an enterprise and its stakeholders. Traidcraft is clear that the interests of all its stakeholders have to be taken into account. This is in a context where many chief executives of major corporations are worshipping at the altar of shareholder value. They are spurred on by both the threatening stick of hostile take-over and the juicy carrot of remuneration arrangements linked to shareholder value creation. This is not to say that the interests of all stakeholders are or should be equal: in Traidcraft's case it is the interests of the poor producers and beneficiaries from our activities that are primary. Rather it is to insist that an organisation has responsibilities to all its stakeholders, and so should be prepared to report to them accordingly.

In Christian thinking, even after Jesus' resurrection, there were and are many *not yets* until this age is brought to an end. We see many signs of hope and encouragement, but still there are frustrations and limitations. This is the story of the church in the New Testament period and for two millennia since; it is also the story of Traidcraft up to now and indeed in whatever its future will be. For the good news about Jesus is that though he was rich, nevertheless for the sake of us humans he became poor, gave up his power and lived amongst ordinary folk as one of us. So as a *Christian* response to poverty, Traidcraft will be an organisation which identifies and participates with the poor; and just as Jesus achieved change in the lives of others at a cost to himself, so the changes which Traidcraft seeks to make to address poverty will be costly. Whatever costs there may be, the God revealed and expressed in Jesus is one who brings life and hope, even through death. So whatever trauma Traidcraft may experience in the years ahead, through it all the God who inspired its inception will be working for good.

TRAIDCRAFT'S PEOPLE: A NETWORK OF RELATIONSHIPS

One of the delights of being involved with Traidcraft is the way it combines both practical and physical realities, such as the importing and distributing of fairly traded products, with the more intangible and virtual realities of influencing the way others think and act. So the organisation's relationships reflect this spectrum of activities. A long-standing dynamic exists within Traidcraft between the doers and the influencers. So for some, the true essence of fair trading is direct participation in undertaking acts of trading fairly directly with producers living in poverty; for others, the real significance of fair trade work is in the wider changes which it brings about. Combining the two in creative and constructive ways is at the heart of Traidcraft's overall mission.

Relationships in the future, even those engaged with the distribution of physical goods, will revolve more around electronic technology, for example as e-commerce penetrates more aspects of commercial activity. Developing relationships between Traidcraft and its various stakeholders in that kind of emerging world will present challenges we have yet fully to comprehend. There are exciting opportunities to develop more direct links and relationships between consumers and producers, or to enable producers to participate directly in lobbying and advocacy work; but there are also risks of losing the sense of relatedness which can be more fully expressed through direct encounter with another person. Placing your order through clicks on a web page creates a different relationship to that fostered through talking face-to-face with your local fair trader at their stall.

Traidcraft functions as a channel, not just for knowledge and goods, but also for human endeavour and voluntary effort. Its work enables donors and staff, shareholders and fair traders, to channel their determination to fight poverty through trade into an effective vehicle for change. Keeping this web of relationships healthy in a fair trade business is no mean feat: Traidcraft's original Foundation Principles acknowledge this, in looking for an approach to trading which will 'not exploit customers by depending on their goodwill to excuse poor service.'

There are several external networks to which Traidcraft relates. Firstly, there are other fair trade organisations: the Fair Trade Foundation, Oxfam's Fair Trade operation, Twin Trading, Equal Exchange, cafédirect, EFTA (European Fair Trade Association), IFAT (International Federation for Alternative Trade), and many others. Secondly, there are other Christian organisations which are also engaged in overcoming poverty and which see fair trade as an important part of that battle: Christian Aid, CAFOD (Catholic Fund for Overseas Development), Tearfund and its Tearcraft business, for example. Thirdly, there are like-minded organisations engaged in different but compatible activities: these include Shared Interest, the

Ethical Trading Initiative whose members include many 'mainstream' businesses, and even the UK government's Department for International Development. Traidcraft's links with all these are of significance, and developing healthy relationships within these networks will increase their capacity to be effective. Sometimes it seems easier and quicker to proceed alone, but constructive relationships between Traidcraft and these other organisations can achieve more effective results and greater influence. As Jesus' followers found, bringing good news to the poor creates tensions amongst those who bring it and these can even undermine the authenticity of the message. So a key principle for Traidcraft is continually to seek to express in the way it operates the values and principles which it advocates in the wider world.

Perhaps the critical test of this integrity of approach came for Jesus in the way he treated those who opposed and ultimately executed him. Even before facing that test, he had taught his followers that the way they treated their enemies would demonstrate their adherence to his radical way of living. So for Traidcraft, how we treat those who oppose fair trade, who seem to us to uphold injustice and benefit from it, may test us to the limits. Sometimes it is the active opponents who present the greatest challenge, but often it is those who unintentionally uphold unjust structures and practices by their passive participation in them who stimulate the most frustration and even anger. Finding good ways to build relationships with them, relationships in which we can challenge as well as dialogue, will be vital if we are to change the world for the better for people living and working in poverty, rather than merely express our indignation to no avail.

Finally, there is another dimension to Traidcraft's understanding of its relationships: God is an active participant, not an absent guest. The resurrection of Jesus demonstrates that God continues to be active in the world he designed and brought into being. In the physical absence of God in human form as he was in Jesus, his Spirit's activity is expressed in many ways: sometimes explicitly and deliberately through the actions of Christians, at other times inclusively through those whose actions serve the Kingdom of God despite their own ambivalence or denial of God's involvement in what they do. Traidcraft seeks to be an organisation through which God's activity in the world can be channelled, embracing the contribution of those who share a Christian faith and those who do not.

TRAIDCRAFT'S PERFORMANCE: RESULTS THAT MAKE A DIFFERENCE

It is the contention of this book that Traidcraft has been able to make a positive difference to the lives of many thousands of producers and workers living in poverty and to the attitudes and practices of many more western citizens and consumers. After more than two decades, what further difference can Traidcraft make? What are the biggest performance challenges that lie ahead?

A Christian vision of the future is one that is both open to real participation by human agents and yet ultimately under the direction and within the control of God. This is in contrast to a deterministic model of the world in which the pervasive hand of random chance determines everything. This Christian vision of an openness to the future has parallels with markets: their day-to-day operation is determined by the independent actions of those who participate in them, yet their activities can be modelled (for example mathematically) and they can be seen to have operated within certain parameters. Take the market for a commodity such as coffee: its price falls within certain boundaries, from something above zero at the bottom to an upper limit which may vary over time. Within those boundaries the price can move rapidly and often unpredictably in response to the actions of consumers, producers and merchants, and the actual and anticipated effects of the weather and other natural phenomena. The actions of supporters of fair trade can make a difference to the operation of the coffee market, and to the price of coffee, initially let us say for those producers who supply cafédirect, but eventually to all producers.

Traidcraft works with participants in markets, and engages as a participant itself. In line with a Christian vision of there being an openness about the future, Traidcraft's participation in markets can make a real difference to the future development of those markets. The implication of this is that Traidcraft's performance in all its activities really matters, working within a Christian vision in which the overall outcome for all creation is within God's intention and decision, but within that framework the detail of the world's future is not a foregone conclusion. In the context of a dynamic rather than static view of the future, humans exercise real choices that have real consequences, and so make a real difference. Indeed, participation in creating the future is part of what living as a consumer, producer, worker or whatever, is all about.

A key aim of Traidcraft's performance is the extent to which people living in poverty are enabled to have increased freedom to participate in markets. This extension of their freedom is intrinsic to development, which extends beyond economic freedoms but which is facilitated by greater economic freedom. Traidcraft's Christian basis means that we do not see material advancement as the sole or even the principal determinant of human well-being; but we do 'regard the existence of gross material inequalities between peoples as a condition to be remedied through the economic system and not perpetuated by it' to quote Traidcraft's original Foundation Principles.[1] So the results that we strive to achieve involve working for change in the way trading activities operate, so that they address poverty rather than exacerbating it. This applies to the trading activities which Traidcraft plc itself undertakes, to the work to support trading by producers that Traidcraft Exchange does, and to the work in which the whole organisation participates to influence the activities of consumers, commercial enterprises, governments and others.

Looking to the future, the power of consumers will continue to have a determining influence on the behaviour of those who supply goods and services to them. So Traidcraft will continue to work to change the demands which consumers make about the basis on which the things they buy have been produced and supplied. There are, however, other powerful influences on the behaviour of corporations and other players in the world of trade. These include the concerns of pension scheme trustees who form a substantial part of the shareholder base of many companies; the legal duties of directors of companies as set down in government legislation; the requirements of the work-ers who staff organisations; and so on. So Traidcraft is also involved in some of these areas which impact so heavily on the conduct of international trade.

The future of trading will also be influenced by the develop-ment of the internet and associated technologies. So as retailers increasingly become e-tailers there will be new dynamics which impact on the position of primary producers, and Traid-craft will need to devise ways to anticipate and respond to these. As the provision of services takes up an increasing proportion of spending, especially amongst relatively well-off westerners, Traidcraft will have to consider what role it might best play, for example in ethical tourism. We can be sure that there will be developments ahead which we cannot identify now: the challenge to Traidcraft will be to maintain the flexibility to change in a changing world, while protecting its network of relationships.

CONCLUSION

The future is uncertain, and so potentially creates fear whether of failure or of insignificance. The Christian gospel proclaims a future of hope and new life. Yet the hope found in Jesus' resur-rection came only after the loss of a painful death: God's way of overcoming was through such suffering rather than by escaping from it. So Traidcraft should not expect to be immune from the challenges of engaging in commercial enterprise or charitable work. Indeed, Traidcraft faces the added difficulties of its cho-sen activities being in the field of fair trade, with all the added complexities which go with that. Moreover, as a Christian response to poverty, there are likely to be times when Traidcraft faces obstacles that a wholly secular organisation would not.

On the other hand, Traidcraft also enjoys benefits from being a value-driven organisation: loyalty and commitment from fair traders, donors, staff, customers, shareholders and others, which would not be created by a purely commercial enterprise in the same way. In addition, the participation of many of those who are Christians amongst its various stakeholders is stimu-lated and sustained by their involvement with Traidcraft being an expression of their faith. The one who raised Jesus from death is a God of surprises, and so we can never be sure what unknown possibilities there may be ahead.

Whatever our own individual relationship to Traidcraft, our involvement and participation can be part of our response to the world in which we live. We are each able to play a part, bringing our hopes and dreams, and so contribute to shaping the future.

NOTES

1   These were revised in 1999 and are reproduced in Appendix Two.

Appendix One

What is Traidcraft?

Traidcraft was founded in 1979 as a Christian response to poverty. It is based on the belief that Christian faith and practice can and should make a difference to the way we engage in trade, and that it is possible to engage in the market place as a commercially viable business, while also ensuring a fair deal for those from the Two-Thirds World who are seeking to sell their products in the international market.

Traidcraft operates on the principle that paying a fair price for products, building the skills capacity and market knowledge of producers and establishing long term relationships of partnership and co-operation, helps poor communities to work their way out of poverty and creates a more equitable world. Most of Traidcraft's trading partners are community-based enterprises and associations of small holder farmers organised for the benefit of their producers and growers. Traidcraft works in partnership with local marketing and capacity building organisations operating with similar values.

Traidcraft is a founder shareholder in cafédirect Limited and is a member of the FairTrade Foundation, the International Federation for Alternative Trade and the European Fair Trade Association. Traidcraft also set up Shared Interest as a savings scheme that enables people to make their savings available as loans to Two-Thirds World producers. It also pioneered social accounting as a means of evaluating a company's performance in a way that goes beyond the bottom line.

HOW IS TRAIDCRAFT ORGANISED?

Traidcraft, the organisation, comprises three bodies:
- *Traidcraft plc* – a trading company operating on fair trade

principles and marketing fair trade products to consumers and distributors in the UK. An important element of Traidcraft plc's sales comes from its relationship with its Fair Trader sales force. In 1999/2000 Traidcraft plc had sales of £7.5 million providing income benefits to more than 80,000 producers and their families across 25 countries.

- *Traidcraft Exchange* is a development charity providing capacity building and market information services to producers and intermediaries, and which is also engaged in awareness-raising activity and the promotion of ethical business practice.
- Both of the above bodies, which are directed by a single management team and Board, are ultimately controlled by the *Traidcraft Foundation*, a registered charity.

Traidcraft's Foundation Principles (in Appendix Two) set out the standards to which Traidcraft aspires. Contact information is given on the final page.

Appendix Two

Traidcraft's Foundation Principles
(revised 1999)

TRAIDCRAFT IS A CHRISTIAN RESPONSE TO POVERTY

Enforced poverty is a gross affront to both the goodness of God as creator in providing for all his creatures and the well-being of human beings. An appropriate Christian response will be marked by:

- a partnership between rich and poor;
- positively affirming the call to all people to steward and develop the creation;
- service, equity and justice which address both persons and processes in wider society; and
- a bias to the poor.

TRAIDCRAFT STRIVES TO SHOW A BIAS TO THE POOR

God is fair to all, so that in the unfairness of the world, his fairness requires a readjustment of many relationships in the world.

The good news of the Kingdom of God brought by Jesus Christ is good news to the poor. Its meaning for everyone is defined by what it means to the poor who receive it. The Kingdom fulfils God's purposes in creation. It needs to come to the poor as good news in their situation, as dignity for the excluded, release for prisoners, recovery of sight for the blind, freedom for broken victims, food for the hungry, drink for the thirsty, housing for the stranger, clothing for the naked, support for the ill and visitation for the prisoner.

Therefore, throughout history, authentic Christian discipleship has expressed a bias to the poor as those who suffer most gravely from the consequences of living in a fallen world.

TRAIDCRAFT STRIVES TO RESPECT PEOPLE
AND THE ENVIRONMENT

One of God's purposes in creation is that men and women together be the image of God, called to represent the owner of the earth as manager and tenant, as stewards of the earth's resources. Stewardship requires access to resources, and to decisions about and responsibility for their use. Traidcraft therefore seeks:

- To develop the wholeness of people in their social and spiritual relationships, with God and their neighbours. We show people most respect by seeing them as God sees them, as his image, of infinite value, and called to eternity with him.
- To express an inclusive community of purpose and relationships, acknowledging the Christian precept of love by putting the interests of others before one's own.
- To show respect for producers, employees, customers and donors by offering good value in goods and services and accurate information.
- To show respect for the environment as the home God provides for humanity and awareness of our own mortality. Being a steward of the earth is not just about our use of the earth's resources but about enabling use by others and passing it on to our children.
- To be a faith-based Christian organisation which welcomes partnership with all who share our commitment to fight poverty through trade, whatever their faith commitments, recognising the work of God in Christ in them.
- To respect and listen to the poor.
- To work with partners and producer groups who fulfil most of the following criteria of fairer trade, to encourage and assist groups to own and meet all of them and to apply these criteria as a minimum for its own internal working.

Those engaged in fairer trade will demonstrate the following:

- Commitment to the poor
  - commitment to develop the whole person in the community
  - recognition of the spiritual dimension of human flourishing.
- Be making products which are (now or potentially) commercially viable.

- Be open to examination of their aims, objectives and commercial practices.
- Be engaged in working practices which are characterised by
    - good stewardship of human and material resources
    - fair wages and working conditions that are normally at or above the average in poor communities
    - recognition of each person's worth and the need for their task
    - a good match between each person's task, skills and capabilities
    - adequate facilities and equipment for the task
    - adequate safety precautions
    - opportunity to participate in decisions, associate in free trades unions, and share in the responsibilities and benefits of ownership
    - caring and friendly atmosphere in the workplace
    - pleasant work environment
    - recognition of workload, flexibility to share work and job-share
    - freedom to use skills gained or pay received to go on to further training or other employment.
    - amelioration of work generally agreed to be tedious and unpleasant.
    - respect for the environment.

TRAIDCRAFT SEEKS TO BE TRANSPARENT AND ACCOUNTABLE

Traidcraft will give account of its stewardship by regular reporting to its stakeholders so that they may evaluate Traidcraft by the principles it espouses.

TRAIDCRAFT STRIVES TO SHOW CREATIVITY AND INNOVATION

As children of a creator God we seek to enhance the creative and liberating potential of communities and persons as stewards of creation.

TRAIDCRAFT STRIVES TO BE THE BEST

Our standards of judgement for the best decisions, processes and structures (commercial and otherwise) are those which seek to reflect the standards set by Jesus in his life and teachings. We are challenged by Jesus to be both a lamp on a stand (to give light to society around) and to be yeast in the dough (being closely involved in society). We set ourselves to discover how to be ever more faithful to this calling.

Traidcraft's Contact Addresses

Traidcraft
Kingsway
Team Valley
Gateshead
NE11 0NE

Tel. 0191 491 0591
Fax 0191 482 2690

email: comms@traidcraft.co.uk

Web site: www.traidcraft.co.uk